EUROPEAN
ECONOMIC
INTEGRATION
1815–1970

EUROPEAN ECONOMIC INTEGRATION 1815–1970

SIDNEY POLLARD

with 78 illustrations, 10 in colour

THAMES AND HUDSON · LONDON

1 *Frontispiece*
'Federation, the only way out',
a Dutch poster by Jan Bons, 1948.

Picture research by Georgina Bruckner

Printed and bound in Great Britain by Jarrold and Sons Ltd, Norwich

ISBN 0 500 32031 4 *hardcover*
ISBN 0 500 33031 X *paperback*

CONTENTS

I INDUSTRIALIZATION AND THE GROWTH OF TRADE

The economy of Europe in 1815, at the beginning of the hundred years' peace, was still basically a pre-industrial one. Most people worked on the land, many of them under servile conditions. Industry was carried on by handicraftsmen in small workshops, or by workers in their homes, using simple tools and animal motive power, or wind and water. Most towns were very small, and were little more than market-places for the exchange of the fruits of the soil for manu-factured goods. The larger towns, including the capital cities, were places in which the landed classes spent their rents, and which there-fore showed a concentration of luxury and of service trades, mostly of a traditional kind in which labour was the main input.

Scattered among these small-scale enterprises there were, it is true, larger units, some using complex and costly capital equipment: mines for coal or metals, manufactories of glass or china or textiles, or armaments works. But these were so swamped numerically by the rest of the economy that they could not affect its character. More significantly, there were the ports and the waterways, some of them man-made. Over the centuries, the relatively low costs of transport by water, even over long distances, had permitted Europe to trade not only in costly fabrics and spices, or in products found in limited areas only – like Swedish iron or Cornish tin – but also in bulky produce that was found everywhere, but could be sold more cheaply in some areas than in others – like timber, flax or even grain.

Nevertheless, a man absent since 1750 would, on returning in 1815, have found a great deal of progress in the economic life on the Conti-nent, but, on a superficial inspection, little to astonish him. In Great Britain, however, developments had taken a different turn: a succes-sion of technological inventions, of innovations in the organization and structure of industry and transport, of capital formation and of changes in the forms of employment, had set off an irreversible chain reaction which has come to be known as the Industrial Revolution. Conditions of war, and particularly the blockade which Napoleon and the British government had imposed on each other from 1806

2 Early technical progress in Germany followed by stagnation: a rotating crane operated by treadmill, originally set up at Düsseldorf in 1598 and still in use as late as 1835.

onwards, had seriously interrupted the normal contacts between Britain and the more advanced countries on the Continent. In 1815 the European countries found across the Channel a modern industrial power in a vigorous and expansive phase of its development, ready to swamp them, first with its mass-produced manufactures, and next with the system which had produced them. The history of the following hundred years is in some important ways the history of the expansion of the Industrial Revolution into successive areas of the Continent, with all the concomitant changes which it brought in its train; one of the most important of these was the progressive economic integration of Europe, which forms the subject of this book.

8

It would be wrong to suggest that the development of Europe as an economic entity had to wait for the process of industrialization in the nineteenth century. Records of trade in rare metals, slaves, luxury artefacts, go back to the Roman Empire and beyond, and the great themes of medieval and early modern history, Christianity and its schisms, the migrations of peoples, developments in science and technology, make sense only in a European, not a national context.

By the eighteenth century, many of the factors which were to contribute to industrialization were operating across the whole of Europe, though their concentration in the west of the Continent and their weakening as one proceeded eastward had become notable and was to become increasingly marked after 1815. A common upper-class culture, now using French rather than Latin as its *lingua franca*, provided the basis for the communications and mutual instruction of *savants* and applied scientists across the frontiers. For most of the century technological advances in Britain and France were followed closely in Holland and Prussia and, at some distance, in Saxony, Switzerland, Austria, Spain and elsewhere. It has even been claimed that British and French technology became more closely assimilated to each other in the course of the century as Britain absorbed the facility to manufacture objects of art and beauty while France learnt methods of cheap mass production. The expansion of trade proceeded at a very similar rate in the two countries, as did the growth in pro-duction in some of the leading industries, though both trade and output operated at a higher level per head in Britain than in France.

While in the first half of the century British manufacturers still had much to learn from the Continent – silk-throwing from Italy, cloth-finishing and dyeing and agricultural improvements from Holland, porcelain-making from Germany, paper-making and silk-weaving from France – the acceleration of inventiveness on the British side of the Channel turned the traffic very much in the other direction to-wards the end of the century. Significantly, the French authorities were quick to spot the change and a number of well-equipped agents and private individuals like Gabriel Jars, Marchant de la Houlière, Faujas de Saint-Fond and Guillaume Louis Ternaux came to learn what they could of British methods to apply them at home. Prussia sent von Reden, F.A.A. Eversmann and vom Stein, and there were visitors from Sweden, from Russia and from Austria, Saxony and the minor German states, to England and, indeed to France, looking for ways to keep their own countries in step. 9

L'INDUSTRIEL,

Journal

PRINCIPALEMENT DESTINÉ A RÉPANDRE LES CONNAISSANCES UTILES
A L'INDUSTRIE GÉNÉRALE, AINSI QUE LES DÉCOUVERTES ET LES
PERFECTIONNEMENS DONT ELLE EST JOURNELLEMENT L'OBJET,

RÉDIGÉ PAR M. CHRISTIAN,

DIRECTEUR DU CONSERVATOIRE DES ARTS ET MÉTIERS;

Orné de 18 planches gravées en taille-douce par M. LEBLANC.

Iʳᵉ ANNÉE. — TOME Iᵉʳ.

On souscrit
AU BUREAU DU JOURNAL DU COMMERCE,
Rue Saint-Marc, Nº 10;
ET A LA LIBRAIRIE DE L'INDUSTRIE,
Même Maison.

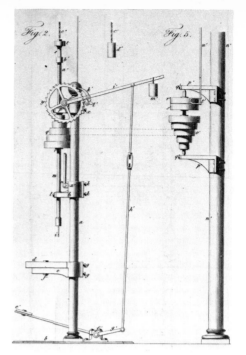

3, 4 *L'Industriel*, a French journal first published in 1826 to disseminate technical information, and a sample illustration showing a new British drill design.

More effective was the transmission of technology by British experts. Apart from the well-known names, like John Kay, John Holker and William Wilkinson, there was a seemingly endless stream of British experts to advise, and to build and manage the new mills, factories, mines and ironworks on the Continent. Thus cotton textiles in France benefited from the work of, among others, John Milne and his sons, machine-builders from Manchester; Morgan, Brown, Lord, Martin, Spenser and Massey at Amiens; Sykes at St Rémy; Wright and Jones at Melun; Wood and Hill at Louviers; Bennett at Grand-Andelys; William Hall, Wilson and Garnett at Rouen; Davis, Morrison, Porter at Bourges; Bettings at Nantes; and the Kelly Brothers and Thomas Clark (Leclerc) at Bourges and elsewhere. Similar aid was received by the Low Countries, Switzerland and several German states, in textiles, in engineering, iron-making by the coke-smelting process, and other innovations. A Watt engine was

5 Copying British technology: a new type of steam-engine being demonstrated before Napoleon III in 1860. ▶

set up in France less than five years after the first prototype was working in England, and it reached Germany soon after; coke-smelting, jenny and mule-spinning, machine-carding, and all the succession of minor improvements which went to make up technical progress, could be found in demonstration models at least, exhibited by British experts and, as likely as not, subsidized by governments or leading public figures, almost as soon as in neighbouring counties of England. It was merely the speed of acceptance that was different on the Continent, despite the energy of local entrepreneurial and mechanical talent.

To the free movement of ideas and of leading innovators has to be added the movement of capital, from its centres in Amsterdam or Frankfurt-on-Main and, increasingly, London. The trade which it financed was also expanding, including not merely shipments of sugar, tea or tobacco to supply the rising consumption of Europe, but also the exchange of goods within Europe, including, significantly, substantial exports of British grain in the first half of the century and growing imports of grain into Britain in its last quarter.

It was precisely because Europe had increasingly come to feel itself, at least culturally, as one world with France as its centre that the revolutionary wars were fought with such bitterness and that Napoleon, in the end, could not rest anywhere along his ambitious road until he had become master of the whole Continent. The war interrupted many existing trade connections, while on the other hand, Napoleon's Continental System may be viewed as an attempt to turn Europe (minus Britain) into a single economy. But underneath

the military and diplomatic comings and goings, the natural streams of commerce went on flowing strongly. The delicate registration of the fluctuating exchange rates achieved in Hamburg during the war, and the massive flow of gold backwards and forwards between England and France in 1793–97 were proofs of an interlinked currency system, just as the inability of the French to stamp out trade with Britain and their ultimate retreat into permitting it under licence may be taken as proof of the vital part which that trade was now playing in the life of Europe.

Many of the frontiers drawn by the Peace of Vienna appeared to be disruptive of some of the most important existing trade links. Thus Belgium and Rhineland-Westphalia, two of the most advanced industrialized areas of Europe, were cut off from the French market which had called them into existence, one to be linked with the small trading and agricultural economy of Holland, the other with the largely agricultural kingdom of Prussia which, though larger in population, was separated from it by a belt of other German states. Northern Italy, where it was not assigned to Austria, was broken into impotent principalities. And the two great empires of the east, Austria and Russia, retreated behind rising tariff walls which the progress of the years allowed them to administer with growing effectiveness. To crown all, the devastating post-war commercial crisis in Britain and the easy peacetime conditions of transport allowed Britain's superior mechanized industry, particularly the makers of cotton and woollen textiles, of yarns and iron goods, to flood the continental markets in the years 1815–20; this had the effect of strangling many promising industrial firms at birth and releasing a revulsion against British imports in many countries which found expression in the erection or strengthening of high protective tariff barriers.

The omens therefore seemed to be pointing towards a reversal of the previous trend, and towards a break-up of the European economy. In fact, the exact opposite occurred, and the trend towards integration not only continued but took on a new dimension. The most obvious and tangible expression of economic interdependence was the growth in trade, and it is to that growth in imports and exports between 1815 and 1914 that we must now turn.

It has long been understood that there is a close connection between industrialization and the expansion of foreign trade. An industrializing economy, much more than the traditional society which it replaces, is likely to need large markets for its mass-produced goods, and therefore to seek export outlets for factories where it was once satisfied with bespoke orders for workshops. It is likely, at the same time, to have to import at least some of the raw materials or fuels or building materials in proportion to its expanding industrial sector. The transfer of labour from agriculture to industry and the parallel technical improvements in agriculture, often associated with specialization, are likely to lead to a demand for food imports, and the rising incomes of the population will be spent in part on imports of all kinds. At the highest level, some specialized manufactures, and services such as banking and insurance, may obtain a world-wide market. It is, in fact, one of the features of industrialization that the proportion of manufactured goods, traded among the advanced nations themselves, rises as a result of specialized demands for fashion, brand names and refined differences of taste. These effects are likely to be more powerful among the smaller countries than among the larger, variegated economies such as Britain, France and Germany, and will be more than proportionally increased by the population growth which usually accompanies industrialization, and which was certainly a major feature of the industrial revolutions in Europe in the period 1815–1914. Conversely, industrialization in many countries has been assisted and perhaps even called into being by opportunities to export.

The effects, however, are not all one way: thus, an industrializing country may learn to make what it formerly imported, and import substitutions of this kind may be highly significant where there is a large home population. In some of the larger and more advanced countries in Europe this effect began to show itself clearly in the twenty years or so before 1914. Further, it may use up, for its own consumption, natural resources, particularly fuel, timber or minerals, which it formerly exported. Alternatively, new techniques may have taught it to substitute materials available at home for others formerly imported. A greater proportion of effort will be devoted to refining and finishing existing products rather than performing similar operations on ever larger quantities of raw materials. After a while, it will also spend more on non-exportable services and, perhaps, on building, so that national income will go up without a parallel rise in trade. Towards the end of the nineteenth century, some protectionist German economists, basing their views on these considerations, even propounded a 'law of diminishing foreign trade' with rising income. However, in the earlier stages of industrialization with which we are mainly concerned here, not only was the growing inter-dependence among countries the predominating tendency, reaching its high point in 1870–1914, but it was precisely this opportunity to export to the less industrialized world which added momentum to the expansion of the new industries, and which became the main force in transmitting the process itself from the centre, first to neighbouring regions in western Europe, and then to the periphery and to overseas territories. Unlike some twentieth-century examples, the industrializing countries of Europe were not converted to industrialization, they were simply permeated by it.

Evidence for this growing economic interpenetration in nineteenth-century Europe may be found in the statistics of imports and exports among the leading countries. In every case, the ratio of foreign trade to national income rose with the rise in incomes and in manufacturing output, and recent research has shown that this relationship can be established in space as well as in time; thus, at any time, the more advanced countries show a higher dependence on foreign trade than the less industrialized ones, in rough order of their state of progress, if allowance is made for their size.

For the world as a whole, it has been estimated that while production per head between 1800 and 1913 grew by less than two and a quarter times, foreign trade per head grew over twenty-five times; or putting it another way, while the world proportion of foreign trade to production was 33 per cent in 1913, it was only 3 per cent in 1800. The period of fastest growth was between 1820 and 1880. For Europe alone, the increase was less dramatic since the level of trade was much higher at the beginning of the period. For the United Kingdom, trade (imports plus exports) as a proportion of national income rose from 14 per cent early in the eighteenth century to 27 per cent at the beginning of the nineteenth, and after staying at that level until the 1840s, rose to about 45–50 per cent by the 1860s, and to 55–60 per cent in the last decade before 1914. In France, the proportion rose from 10 per cent at the beginning of the nineteenth century to 25–35 per cent in the period 1872–1914. In Germany, the ratios rose from 13 per cent in 1840 to 30–38 per cent by the latter end of the period; in Italy, from 10 per cent in 1830 to 20–28 per cent towards the end; and in Sweden, from 28 per cent in the 1860s to 40 per cent by 1911–13. No reliable sources going back for more than a few decades exist for other countries, but the indications are that in their case, too, industrialization was accompanied by a similar rise of the

14

foreign trade component, also stabilizing at a high level by the end of the period as the counteracting tendencies of import substitution and autarky came into play.

Such statistics, impressive though they are, tend to understate the tendency for the integration of the European economy for at least two reasons. First, the percentage is measured against a total of national income which is itself rapidly growing with industrialization and the population increase accompanying it. In Great Britain, for example, between 1815 and 1914, population increased threefold, national income tenfold and foreign trade nearly twentyfold. Between 1830 and 1910, foreign trade per head rose twelvefold in France, over tenfold in Germany, Belgium, Spain and Portugal, ninefold in Italy, eightfold in Sweden and Norway, sevenfold in Austria, fourfold in Russia, where industrialization was not yet complete, and by no less than fourteen and a half times in Holland.

Secondly, however, these figures conceal the dynamic and operational nature of the international trade of European countries in this period. European nations were exporting not only commodities and services, but capital, people, ideas and entrepreneurship: in a very real sense they were exporting the Industrial Revolution to each other. Some of these aspects will be dealt with in later chapters. The remainder of this chapter will be devoted to a description, in broad outline, of this interlocking development of the spread of industrialization and economic integration in Europe.

Three phases can usefully be distinguished. In the first, from 1815 to the mid-century, Britain dominated developments as the only mature industrial economy to have emerged from the long years of war. Her manufactured exports swamped most of Scandinavia, Germany and the Mediterranean countries: 'The British', according to Talleyrand, French ambassador in Naples, referring to the 1830s, 'know how to put themselves out to meet the needs, the whims and the imagination of men, making for them fabrics at all kinds of prices according to the state of poverty of the regions for which they are intended.' Only France, Russia and Austria succeeded in keeping out the flood of mass-produced goods by means of high tariffs, and even then there was much smuggling in the east, while in France fashions became 'anglo-maniac', and Paris tailors were reported as visiting London regularly to buy their lastings, stuffs and cloths there.

This European market was of fundamental importance to British industrialization, which would have been substantially retarded without

15

6 Secure in her competitive trading superiority, Britain could afford to dismantle her protective system, as shown in this *Punch* cartoon of 1846 looking several years ahead; the final steps in the process were the repeal of the Corn Laws (1846) and of the Navigation Acts (1849).

THE BRITISH LION IN 1850;

OR, THE EFFECTS OF FREE TRADE.

it. In 1816–22 Europe took almost 60 per cent of all British exports, mainly manufactures and coal, and it still took 51 per cent in 1829-30; in addition Europe was the main market for British re-exports of colonial goods. The German states formed the chief market, other major trading partners being Russia, France, the Netherlands, Italy, Turkey and Greece. Yet this trade, vital to Britain, proved to be of equal importance in the long run to her continental customers. For while in 1830 Britain sold half her exports to Europe, she also took a third of her imports thence. It is true that most of these consisted of food and raw materials, grain and wool, timber and naval stores, minerals, dried fruit and wines, and this, at first sight, looks like a 'colonial' pattern of trade, the benefits of which go mainly to the industrial partner, while the development of the primary producer is held in check. It is, however, crucial for an understanding of European history to bear in mind that large parts of Europe were by no means underdeveloped or colonial in the modern sense. Their income per head, their long-standing accumulation and use of capital, their legal and cultural traditions, and their industrial technology were not in the least inferior to those of Britain when the latter 'took off' into industrialization in the late eighteenth century. In those areas, therefore, little more than precept and a trigger were needed to propel them forward also.

It is in this light that we have to see the market provided by Britain to the agrarian classes of Europe which were capable of responding to commercial opportunities to increase their saleable surpluses. In every European country, an agricultural revolution has accompanied or preceded the Industrial Revolution, and while the home population growth provided a major stimulus in this period, the British market provided another. Nowhere is this clearer than in the history of the German Zollverein (Customs Union, formed in 1834), which in the first thirty years of its existence increased its exports of meat and meat products by 50 per cent, doubled its exports of wheat, increased its exports of sugar more than sixfold and multiplied its exports of spirits eightfold, while laying the foundations of the most successful industrial economy on the European continent. In a very similar light of helping rather than retarding must be seen the British investments on the Continent; these did not serve to perpetuate the economic dependence of the rest of Europe, but rather, wherever conditions were ripe, to provide the critical initial support for modern industry or transport which might not have been forthcoming otherwise. This topic is treated at greater length in Chapter III.

Beyond this, economic progress in Europe was built up on a shifting system of complementarity which continuously changed and adapted in accordance with resources and comparative costs. Thus industrialization in Britain stimulated not only Prussian agriculture, and with it transport, including docks and railways, in the period 1815–50; cheap British yarn also stimulated Prussian cotton-weaving, where the technical superiority of Britain was less marked and lower German wages formed a more significant proportion of costs so that Britain exported diminishing quantities of fabrics to the Zollverein, but rising quantities of yarn: whereas in 1820 Europe still took 51 per cent of British cotton piece-goods, the proportion in 1850 had dropped to 16 per cent and in 1880 to 8 per cent, while in the same years the share of Asia, Africa and Australia had risen from 17 to 49 and finally 75 per cent. On the basis of cheap British yarns, Prussian and Swiss weavers and Saxon knitters and lacemakers could now begin to swamp markets in Russia, Italy and the rest of Germany. In turn, these regions were able to use the resources now available to them to develop their own economies on the basis of low-cost imports and consequent export opportunities. Gradually, as German

17

7–10 Advertisements reflecting the rise of international trade and the migration of manufacturers. Right, German textiles advertised in Bulgaria, 1894; below left, British steam-engines and machinery advertised in Germany, 1870; below right, a German engineering firm of British origin trading in Bulgaria, 1894; opposite, a German precision engineering firm advertising in Britain, 1900.

mills would learn to spin their own yarn, Britain would sell them machines to make yarn, and in the next phase, machines to make machines, while both countries could now turn outward to sell their fabrics and yarns to less developed ones, where in due course a similar process would begin. In the case of woollen goods Germany in fact kept most of her capacity to make coarse goods and export them to the east and south, while taking finer woollen and worsted fabrics from England. In the case of linen, too, the spinning went to Britain while, in this phase, the weaving stayed on the Continent.

Far from killing all native manufacture, therefore, Britain called forth a great deal of complementary industrial capacity, of the domestic type in the first instance, while also laying the solid foundations for later mechanization and at the same time encouraging the creation of vital social overhead capital, and of new markets in the east, as western Europe was being flooded by Britain. Continental industrialists learnt to live with the new conditions, and to use them as spring-boards for the next stage. As long as the industrialized centre – in this early phase, Britain almost exclusively – was willing to permit imports to flow in and capital to flow out, the virtuous circle of mutual stimulation and economic growth could continue.

11 An idealized view of industry in Germany. This picture, to illustrate a
Nuremberg engineering works and foundry in 1858, features allegories of

The infant industrial centres thus raised up were concentrated in a
few limited geographical areas. The most important lay along a
discontinuous narrow salient, pointing to the heart of Europe from
the coast opposite Great Britain, with the Rhine valley (which was
still the main route of entry for British goods into Europe) as its centre
line. It included Flanders, the northern French and Belgian coal-field,
Rhineland-Westphalia, Alsace and parts of Switzerland. A second
area consisted of a belt of valleys stretching across Saxony, Upper
Silesia and Bohemia. Other centres were to be found along the Seine
and in Paris, along the Danube valley above and below Vienna,
around St Petersburg, and in the valleys around Lyons and St Etienne.
Surrounding these centres of advanced industrialization and com-
mercialization was a penumbra of territories which, although not
yet developed to the same extent, yet had the income levels, the trade

steam, physics, mathematics, industry, commerce and trade, together with others representing morning, evening and the city of Nuremberg.

links, the industrial and handicraft population, the natural resources and the legal freedom to react without much delay to positive stimuli. This area might be broadly defined as lying west of a line drawn along the Elbe and south to the tip of the Adriatic, and north of a line drawn through Rome, Barcelona and Santander. Parts of Scandinavia and Poland would also have to be included.

By the late 1840s the smaller core areas were not only in many respects as advanced as comparable regions in Britain: they had also, in turn, become in effect new suns of new solar systems radiating outwards their exports of manufactures and capital, of skill and of enterprise, to awaken still new areas. Belgium, developed in part by such engineers as the Cockerills, J. Bell or Duncan and Grant, with a railway system that owed a great deal to British enterprise and design and to French and British capital, had become, in turn, a centre for the

21

diffusion of machines, technology and manufactures into much of the rest of Europe. There was a well-developed coal-field, there was an old-established textile industry, there was one of the most advanced agricultural regions in Europe, and there were advanced engineering centres in Ghent, Malines, Brussels, Tirlemont, Liège, Verviers and Seraing. Typically, in 1830, 21 per cent of Belgium's steam-engines were foreign, and at the end of 1844, just over 10 per cent; in 1839, one-third of railway locomotives were foreign built. In the 1830s Belgium nevertheless exported steam-engines with a total value seven times greater than that of the engines she imported, and Belgian-made engines were to be found all over Germany, Austria and even further afield.

'John Cockerill', it was said in 1835, 'travels on the great highways in his coach. Here he builds furnaces and there chimney stacks. He covers fields with his tents and then when all the preparations have been made he erects the steam engines which have followed in his wake . . . And John Cockerill climbs back into his coach and government officials unsuspectingly sign his passport as if it referred to a consignment of wine and they do not realise that this silent man who seldom puts pen to paper is far more likely to turn their old world upside down than many a revolutionary who has his pockets stuffed with political programmes and manifestoes.'*

Northern France developed her ironworks, smelting with coke, and in the traditional textile areas, in the north-west, north and in Alsace, output took a sharp upward turn after the dislocations of the post-war years. Between 1829 and the end of the 1840s, French exports of woollen goods increased by three and a half times, of cottons nearly three times, of silk by half, while the export of linen goods fell; French consumption of raw cotton was one-third of the British, but as France produced goods of higher quality, the value of her output has been estimated at 60 per cent of the British. Alsace became a centre of textile-machinery engineering and invention of international importance, supplying manufacturers in France, Switzerland and Germany; and textile mills along the Rhine and in Saxony were beginning to install spinning machines of the latest design. French exports consisted of manufactures to the extent of three-quarters, mainly to Mediterranean countries and the USA, as well as to the rest of Europe, while over two-thirds of her imports consisted of materials needed in industry, and only one-tenth of manufactures.

* Translated in W.O. Henderson, *Britain and Industrial Europe, 1750–1870* (Leicester, 1965), p. 130

The states of Germany as a whole were still primarily producers and exporters of food and raw materials, but the foci of industrial development were advancing rapidly: thus Prussian coal production rose by 6–7 per cent a year in 1830–45, German pig-iron output rose by 10 per cent a year in 1830–40 and accelerated later with the building of the railway network, while the number of cotton-mills in Saxony rose from 91 in 1834 to 130 in 1837. In both countries, as in Belgium, Austria and elsewhere, the concentration of capital and the spread of the joint-stock form of organization were particularly marked in the development of the railways.

Thus the years 1815–50 had seen the opening up and penetration of Europe by British mass-produced manufactures, but at the same time also the creation in a number of favoured centres of a modern industrial base. By the end of the period, those centres had become sufficiently well equipped with modern technology and capital, with entrepreneurship and a skilled and amenable labour force, not merely to supply less developed regions of Europe and the world, but even to compete with Britain in a few select areas, and to 'colonize' in turn, other parts of Europe in which favourable conditions existed for the new industrialism.

The second phase, from *c.* 1850 to the boom in 1873, saw what was probably the fastest rate of expansion of European industry and investment. Britain, the first focus of the Industrial Revolution, having laid the foundation, now began to be slowly pushed out of all parts of Europe as far as her manufactured goods were concerned, though she still supplied capital goods and re-exported colonial produce. Her prodigious efforts of capital investment and sales of manufactures abroad were now largely diverted towards overseas 'areas of recent settlement', like the USA and Australia, and to colonies like India. The share of British exports going to Europe fell from about 50 per cent in 1850 to 40 per cent in 1870–74, while exports to British possessions had risen to 25·6 per cent by the latter date. It has been calculated that between 1848 and 1877 Britain exported no less than £800 million worth of capital goods, and drove out almost all competition in the world's shipping industry. In fact it became Britain's particular role in this period to open up sources of supply of food and raw materials from hitherto inaccessible or underdeveloped regions overseas for the use of the whole of industrial Europe, with France playing a secondary part in this, mainly in countries bordering on the Mediterranean. A new world-wide triangular trade and balancing pattern tended to develop, in which the Continent as a whole had a surplus with Britain, Britain had a surplus with the overseas primary producers, and they in turn registered a surplus with the continent of Europe. In place of Britain, Franco-Belgian capital, from the second European focus, now took over the role of developing not only the resources of France, but also those of other promising areas in Europe, like western Germany, Austria, Italy and Spain, as well as Egypt which attracted investors by the promise of cotton supplies during the cotton famine of the American Civil War period, and the challenge of the Suez Canal, finally opened in 1869. At the same time, tertiary centres, particularly in Germany, were preparing to develop their own territories, primarily within the Zollverein, but also to move outward to their less developed neighbours with their potential markets in the east and south-east. Thus between 1836–40 and 1861–64, while Zollverein exports of food rose by about two and a half times in volume, the export of manufactures rose by over three times, and of minerals, sevenfold.

None of these developments showed any signs of a 'forced' growth imposed from outside. On the contrary, they were building on the foundations of centuries of slow accumulation of capital, technical skills, capitalistic attitudes and wage labour. Within the similar framework of the new industrial capitalism the entrepreneurs of each region learnt to adapt their available factors of production, thus laying in this period the foundations of a growing division of labour in Europe, which was based not so much on the stage of development reached, as in the first half of the century, but on the resource endowment of the area: the coal of Upper Silesia, the Ruhr, or Belgium-northern France; the water-power of Switzerland; the timber and iron ore·of Sweden; or the old-established industrial and commercial skills in the use of imported raw materials in Holland or Italy.

13 A centre of German industry and scientific research: an aniline and soda works at Ludwigshafen in 1881, later to become part of one of the giants of the chemical industry in Germany.

Meanwhile in the areas outside the penumbra of the late industrializers, where there had been little or no preparation in past centuries for industrialization, the foundations began to be laid for at least the preparatory stages: serfdom was abolished in Austria-Hungary and in Russia, and the abolition of serfdom given a clothing of reality in the eastern provinces of Prussia; entry into the trades and professions was opened to the talents, the legal disabilities of the non-noble population to some extent reduced. Anyone could now legally enter any profession, settle anywhere or buy land. Again these developments were not independent of the industrialization in the west, but were called forth directly by the example, the manufactured exports, the capital and the entrepreneurship coming from there. In particular, the growing markets offered for Russian and Hungarian grain and other produce of the periphery served directly to provide a stimulus and new resources for agricultural improvements and for developing railways, docks, service and processing industries, as the first stages of industrialization there.

The second phase, then, was marked by the sturdy growth of the more advanced centres of Europe, largely to take Britain's place, as foci for European industrialization, setting off in turn reactions

25

◀ 12 An American hand-operated seeding machine, as illustrated in an advertisement published in a Hungarian journal in 1868.

between themselves and the areas which had now become the periphery similar to those set up in the earlier phase between Britain and themselves. The Industrial Revolution was, as it were, spreading in ever widening circles, using, in each phase, the newer technologies which had meanwhile been introduced. This phase is dominated by the building up of a railway network in the more advanced regions of Europe. Relatively speaking, the involvement of Britain in European trade grew less in this period (though in absolute terms it was still expanding very rapidly), but the growing preoccupation of Britain with the overseas world did not mean that she was turning her back on the Continent. On the contrary, she became, if anything, even more an integral part of Europe as she developed and linked up vast new areas supplying materials and foodstuffs for the growing industrial complex in Europe as a whole.

In the third phase, from *c.* 1873 to 1914, a number of European centres reached equality, or even overtook, the formerly leading centres of Britain, at what had become much higher levels of output, capital provision and technology. The Ruhr, Upper Silesia, Saxony, the Berlin area, Lorraine-Saar, Alsace, Belgium, the Paris basin, Lyons, the Donetz, Bohemia, Upper and Lower Austria, Lombardy and many lesser areas had now become fully mature industrialized economies. The economic interrelationships increasingly significant for Europe were therefore not merely those of advanced centre to dependent periphery, but also those among the advanced economies.

Even the relationships of the traditional kind, between the industrialized economy and its less developed markets and suppliers, showed new features in this period, for at least two reasons. First, the technological gap to be bridged by the territory newly opened up was constantly widening and becoming less and less easy to span from native resources. For people without previous experience it was a very different matter to construct, for example, an up-to-date complex blast-furnace of the 1900 type from what it had been to put up the relatively simple type of 1830. It was therefore necessary, not merely to supply models or send a few mechanics, as had been done earlier in the century, but to export and maintain for long periods complex capital equipment in the parts of Europe to be developed. Further, instead of a small stream or a local coal supply which might have sufficed to keep the works of 1820 going, modern works might require a battery of ancillary services, supply and repair stations and transport facilities, which would also have to be provided by the advanced countries in the first instance. This, in turn, required much larger initial investments in capital, unlikely to be found locally and therefore necessarily drawn from the industrialized societies, either directly or via the aid of the governments of the developing countries.

Secondly, as industrialization was pushing out further and further from its points of origin in north-western Europe, it was pushing into soil that was less and less well prepared to receive the new seeds fruitfully. Instead of a long history of a capitalist money economy and commercial capitalism, there was recent serfdom, instead of vigorous urban life, there was a largely rural population, and instead of constitutional bourgeois-democratic government there was a corrupt and incompetent autocracy. Instead of providing opportunities for the peasants of these outer areas, the markets and resources of the west ensured their intensified oppression and exploitation, at least for a time. The chances of effective pump-priming, the chances of initiating a growth which would then on its own spread across Russia or the Balkans or Spain, as it had spread earlier across France or Belgium or Germany, were therefore very poor, and the dangers of creating enclaves that would be isolated in a stagnant hinterland, correspondingly greater. It need hardly be stressed that these tendencies have become even more pronounced in the twentieth century, as industrialism, now representing a vastly wider technological gap, is carried into ever less congenial environments outside Europe.

The result was that in this third phase the western countries did not merely export manufactures, but capital equipment, coupled with massive capital exports, and not merely for railways as in the 1850s and 1860s, but also for all kinds of other public utilities and industrial plant itself, requiring supervision and management on a long-term basis. Russia, Turkey or the Balkans became economic colonies in a way which had not applied to France or Germany in their superficially similar stage earlier on. By the same token, countries penetrated a little earlier, like Austria-Hungary or Italy, were still partly in economic thraldom to their sponsors from advanced Europe, while simultaneously becoming colonizers in the Balkans or the Turkish Empire on their own account in the last years before 1914. Italy showed the typical phasing of the west, her manufacturing population rising to an early peak in 1881 but then temporarily falling again, as her earlier domestic manufacture employing much labour ancillary to advanced industry abroad was being replaced by labour-saving factory industry at home.

27

Britain, meanwhile, was confirmed in her move away from Europe and strengthened in her role as the developer, and the go-between, for overseas territories. The share of her total export going to agricultural countries, as opposed to industrial, rose from 56 per cent in 1854–57 to 70 per cent in 1909–13, and the share of her manufactured exports going there, from 59 to 76 per cent. Her imports from 'countries of recent settlement overseas' outside the USA rose from 8 per cent in 1857–59 to 18 per cent in 1911–13, and the share of her capital exports going there, from 10 per cent in 1870 to 45 per cent in 1913.

Economic relationships among the advanced economies had also become very complex. On the one hand, the growing sophistication of consumer demand and of the division of labour among the producers, particularly of capital and engineering goods, had led to an expansion of trade, an intensified commercial interdependence among them. Thus Germany sent to Britain much semi-manufactured steel, and also many sophisticated machines, while Britain sent to Germany finished products. Germany sent electrical machinery to Britain, while importing British agricultural and textile machinery.

28

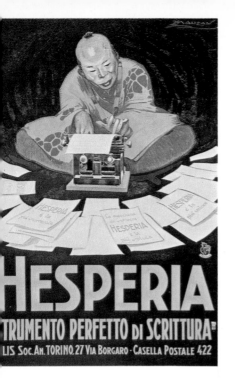

14, 15 Advertisements for
British textile machinery
and the U.S. Singer sewing
machine in Russian trade
directories, 1918 and 1912.

16, 17 Advertisements for
Italian typewriters and
English electric light bulbs,
c. 1900, stressing the world-
wide extent of their
markets.

Britain exported finer textiles, Germany coarser textiles, also cheap watches and clocks – while Switzerland exported expensive ones. More recent industrializers, like Italy and Spain, exported textiles; Sweden exported steel and timber. Not only did this trade in manufactures among the industrialized nations form a major component of world trade; it was also growing faster over much of the period than was the trade in food and raw materials, in spite of growing protectionism. By 1913 the commodity trade between the seven European industrialized countries – Britain, France, Germany, Belgium, Italy, Austria and Switzerland – represented fully one-third of world commodity trade, and of their own exports 51 per cent went to each other. At the same time it should be remembered that in Europe as a whole in 1913 the three largest producers – Britain, France and Germany – with 46 per cent of the population together accounted for the following percentages of total output: coal, 93; steel, 78; machinery, 80; and total manufactures, 72. While in 1880–84 Britain had still held 64 per cent of the machinery exports of the four leading countries, her share had fallen in 1909–13 to 34 per cent, but in absolute values that share had risen from £11·5 million to £32 million.

Throughout this period there was a marked rise in the relative share in production and trade of such capital goods as steel, machinery and vehicles, other metal goods and chemicals, and a fall in the share of consumer goods like food, textiles, clothing and leather goods. This development was so uniform across Europe that the size ratio between these two types of industry has been taken as a measure of the stage of industrialization reached. In part, this differentiation reflects the diminishing share of food and crude raw materials in consumption as personal incomes rise, and in part it reflects the more capital-intensive methods necessary to achieve a rising income. But it is also a result of the particular course taken by the industrialization of Europe and the different phases at which it reached different countries, as described above.

These expanding markets found within the industrialized world between 1873 and 1914 contributed greatly to the growth momentum maintained by the European economy, and to its continued industrialization. Yet it also led to increased friction. As industrialists began to jostle each other in their limited area, they became conscious of the competition between them, and of the fact that while their productive capacity grew, the world that still remained to be opened

18 'Trade and the Empire', a poster illustrating the attitude of Britain to her protectionist neighbours in Europe, *c.* 1900 (cf. illustration 6).

up by them shrank. On 11 October 1880 *The Times* could still write:

'The earth is spacious. For a market closed in one quarter two are opened in another. A regret is pardonable that the neighbours of Great Britain are not very neighbourly in their tariffs. The loss, however, of European custom is redressed as it is, and tends to be more redressed more amply still, by new demands from remoter regions.'

But while the forecast was correct that Britain would find compensation in other continents for the reduced markets in Europe, public opinion was no longer quite as tolerant twenty years later. Capital, commerce and industry are not of their nature nationalistic in outlook, and the period saw a faster growth of the investments of capitalists of one country in the enterprises of another, of international cartels, monopolies and rings, of international labour organizations and of international produce exchanges and banking and exchange facilities, than had ever been seen before. Yet, as the history of Europe in the nineteenth century stood under the influence of growing and victorious nationalism and nation states, the inherent conflict in capitalistic competition became clothed in a national garb. The fact

31

that it was Germans who drove out British exporters from Spain, Italy and Scandinavia and Belgian exporters from Holland, that it was Austrians who clashed with Italians in Balkan railway building, that French, Belgian and German capitalists competed for Russian or Austrian loans and, above all, that the benefits of colonies were to be secured by the rich men of one nation rather than of another, turned the industrial progress of a century of general European peace into a cause for war in 1914.

The growth of protection and of imperialism which materially contributed to this outcome will be discussed in Chapters IV and V. But here we must note one further disruptive element which arose more naturally out of the economic progress of Europe and the world: the changing role of agriculture.

In its early stages the Industrial Revolution, building on agrarian improvements, had been basically beneficial to agrarian interests. On the one hand, a prosperous and growing market was being opened up in the towns and industrial villages; on the other, the shift of population from agriculture into industry raised the marginal product and the incomes of those remaining in agriculture. Given the right stimuli, peasants became market-oriented and specialized, landlords introduced improvements, serfdom was dismantled and governments built or subsidized canals and railways to move the products of agriculture to the market.

In this third phase, however, from the 1870s on, a new element entered into the food markets of Europe: the surpluses of other continents. The investments and migrations of the previous phase were beginning to bear fruit: rail and steamship transport lowered costs and speeded supplies, just as a run of bad harvests in Europe in the second half of the 1870s had softened up European markets. The energies of the American people, released after the Civil War, developed an area almost as big as the fertile regions of Europe. Between 1860 and 1880, while the American population doubled, its output of grain quadrupled. They were soon followed by men in Australia, Canada and the Argentine, who began to develop the

32

20 A German cartoon of Bismarck's tariff of 1879 which arose out of the compact of 'rye and iron'; whips labelled 'protective tariff' are being used to drive forward simultaneously both exports and imports of grain.

agricultural potential of their lands. In Russia, the end of serfdom in the 1860s allowed landlords and tax-gatherers to press more heavily on the peasants, so that an ever larger proportion of the product was turned into cash by being sent abroad, overtaking, early this century, the exports of the USA. Even India and the Danube basin developed a grain surplus which was sent into industrial Europe.

The result was a drastic fall of grain prices, and a substantial fall of prices of other foods. In the United Kingdom, where world prices were permitted to operate freely, the price of wheat (1867–77 = 100) stood at 42 by 1895, beef at 74, pork at 71, mutton at 92, and butter at 74. Although those prices were destined to rise again somewhat by 1914, yet this flooding of the market by cheap food created a trauma for Europe even more severe than the flooding by British manufacturers in 1815–20.

In principle, what was happening was by no means new. Just as the development of Manchester had encouraged agriculture, and ultimately more efficient and low-cost agriculture, in Cheshire, and similar effects could be seen later in the case of, say, the Baltic in relation to the whole of Britain, so, in ever widening circles of mutual dependence, the whole of industrialized Europe was being fed by an ever widening ring of agricultural producers whom it had itself encouraged and financed. Meanwhile, in Europe also agricultural techniques, yields and specialization made rapid progress, but the

33

◀ 19 Advertisement for American preserves in a German journal, 1870.

difference now was that imports came from across frontiers and that political power within and over those frontiers was still held to a disproportionate extent by the landed classes exploiting to the full their surviving historic privileges and influences. This was clearest in Germany, where the traditional Prussian aristocracy, the *Junkers*, had avoided sharing more than a fraction of their power with others. They now managed not only to maintain a tariff on food imports at a level which drastically raised costs for industrialists and lowered consumption standards for workers, but when even that failed to sell for them their inefficiently produced rye (which was increasingly declined by consumers) they designed a most ingenious system of 'import certificates' by which the German consumer and taxpayer actually subsidized them to export that rye, through the mechanism of paying more than necessary for the food which he consumed. Elsewhere, too, wherever landlords dominated, as in Russia and Hungary, or landlords and peasants, as in France and the Balkans, protective barriers were raised against cheap imports of foreign food and encouragement given to home agriculture and its exports.

Yet this was not the only possible answer. In Britain, Belgium, Holland, Switzerland and, most successfully, in Denmark, imports were permitted, but agriculture was switched intelligently to using cheap imported grain, oilcake and other foods to raise meat and dairy produce for which quality and nearness to European urban markets gave a natural advantage. Far from harming agriculture, this more intelligent approach of using an economic rapier instead of a political bludgeon often did much more to help it, as is seen by the comparative wheat yields, expressed in quintals (100 kilograms) per hectare:

		Average yields in	
		1885–89	*1909–13*
Protectionist countries:	Austria	11·1	13·6
	France	11·8	13·2
	Germany	15·3	21·4
	Hungary	12·3	12·6
Free-trade countries:	Denmark	25·6	33·1
	Netherlands	18·8	23·5
	Switzerland	14·1	21·3
	United Kingdom	20·3	21·3

Even in the protectionist countries, the agrarian interests could not hold up the course of history, though they could, as in the case of Germany, direct their agriculture from meat and dairy and similar production, in which it had an economic advantage, into corn-growing, in which it had not. They could not stop Europe's growing dependence on food imports, which was merely a reflection of the growing and successful industrialization. By 1914 the main industrialized countries as a whole imported about one-quarter of their food, even Germany importing well over one-third of the wheat she consumed. The whole of importing Europe, i.e. excluding Russia and the Danubian countries, imported 114 million quintals of corn, out of a total consumption of 400 million, of which up to 40 million came from Russia, and up to 20 million from the Danubian countries.

Nevertheless, agriculture was the most important example in this period for the way in which sectional economic interests, wielding disproportionate political power, could use strident nationalism, sometimes with racist overtones, to disrupt the natural economic advance of Europe and to harm the welfare of their fellow citizens. These interests also helped to condition the European population for the disruption of their economic lives in two world wars separated by a restless period of constant economic warfare.

Thus the third phase, 1873–1914, saw the completion of the growth, in western and central Europe, of a number of mature, industrialized economies which (together with the USA) had turned much of the rest of Europe and the world, less favourably placed for copying the process pioneered in Britain, into a network of supply and market areas. Their own economic interrelationships were still growing in absolute terms, though they had levelled off as a proportion of material income, but it was notable that nationalism, which earlier, by its attack on feudalism and other restrictive privileges, and even by its protection of genuine 'infant' industries, had helped industrialization and economic progress, was now beginning to become a fetter on it.

The century as a whole had seen the economic integration of Europe to a degree unknown and unthinkable before industrialization. The countries affected in succession by the Industrial Revolution did not industrialize independently, growing like plants in separate flower-pots. Their transformation was a single process, the changes in each depending on the stages reached by the others, on the supplies, technologies and markets of its neighbours and the development of the world outside Europe. Though many experiences of industrialization recurred again and again in recognizable patterns, the whole process represented a unique phase in the history of the world.

35

II THE NEW MEANS OF TRANSPORT AND COMMUNICATION

It is an oft-quoted commonplace that travel at the time of Napoleon was no faster than at the time of the Roman Empire, namely at the speed of the fastest relay of horses. What is perhaps of greater significance is that outside the French Empire, the roads were a good deal worse than those of Rome in classical times, and that whatever speed might be maintained by official messengers, ordinary travellers moved much more slowly, and goods more slowly still.

The sorry state of the European road network at the beginning of the nineteenth century was itself a cause of the economic isolation of so many districts, as well as being a symbol of their backwardness, for traffic very soon creates its own roads. France had inherited a splendid system of 'royal' highways, dating from the reign of Louis XIV and built largely for strategic reasons, which excited the envy of visiting foreigners even though long stretches had been allowed to fall into neglect. Napoleon enlarged and improved the system, spending 308 million francs on the roads and another 25 million on bridges between 1807 and 1812, again for strategic reasons, though by abolishing road tolls he also intended to aid internal and international commerce. His roads radiating from Paris over the Simplon and Mont Cenis passes to Switzerland and Italy and across German lands to Hamburg and the high roads to Amsterdam and Madrid, also formed the first major international links of a superior standard. In 1814 there were some 27,000 kilometres (17,000 miles) of 'imperial' roads within France, in addition to the network of local roads.

Elsewhere, however, even that limited system of main strategic highways was missing. The provinces of Germany adjoining France had inherited some of her roads, and in Prussia, of 523 Prussian miles (say 2,500 statute miles) of *chaussée*, or high road which only gradually became macadamized, over three-fifths were in Rhineland-Westphalia in the west. By contrast, the huge provinces of Posen and Pomerania had no *chaussée* at all, while the (province) Prussia possessed a single mile. The post-chaise from Berlin took four days to Breslau and seven

37

21 Symbol of the new means of transport penetrating even backward provinces: the railway station at Rendsburg, Prussia, in 1846.

days to Königsberg, the major provincial capital in the east. South-westward, the first day's journey out of Berlin, starting out at 8 or 9 a.m., and including repeated stops for luggage checks, reached the little town of Belitz late at night only some thirty-five (English) miles away. Yet so small was the demand for improvement, and so different were conditions in Germany from contemporary Britain, that in 1816 President von Vincke could write from Westphalia, the most advanced province, that the inhabitants objected to road improvement, first because they feared that it would invite the passage of troops and the obligation to quarter them; secondly, because innkeepers and tradesmen would lose the custom derived from travellers on the slow roads; and thirdly, 'it was a new thing and so far they had managed to do without'. Von Vincke himself, when opening the Cleve-Mark Diet of 1805, had preferred to walk the twenty miles from Münster to Hamm rather than entrust himself to a wheeled vehicle on the existing roads.

If passenger traffic was slow and laborious, goods traffic was necessarily even more so. The furthest possible distance for transporting timber or grain was about twelve miles: beyond it the cost of freight began to exceed the value of the goods, though cattle on the hoof traversed very long cross-country distances. Again, road transport was even more limited in the peripheral areas of Europe. Thus, in Russia the 'roads' were sandy tracks in the summer, quagmires in the spring and autumn, and only in winter could the hardier souls travel reasonably fast in horse-drawn sleighs. The first main highway, Moscow–St Petersburg, was completed only in 1834.

In the next few decades much effort was devoted to road improvement, particularly in France and Prussia. In France, the work consisted mostly in improving existing roads, mainly the departmental and local ones, and by the 1830s the network was so good that it may have delayed the building of railways. In Prussia the government and the Seehandlung (a kind of royal investment bank) spent 17·5 million *Thaler* on roads 1816–32, in addition to a substantial expenditure by local authorities. Most of this was spent in the west, but there was some effort now also devoted to the economically undeveloped agrarian districts in the east. Even Pomerania, with no main roads in 1816, had 33 (English) miles by 1828. By 1845 Prussia had 6,550 (English) miles of state highways, of which 3,400 were in the western provinces and Silesia, and there were another 1,260 miles of local highways. Meanwhile, the abolition of tolls, octrois (duties) and the obnoxious searches connected with them did as much to speed and cheapen internal transport by road.

Unlike British roads, however, the improved continental road system was destined to play little part in industrialization. The forces calling it into existence operated so much later that road-building was overtaken by the building of the immensely more efficient railways. Again, roads contributed little to strengthening the ties between the different countries of Europe. Much more was accomplished in this direction by waterways and ultimately by railways.

WATERWAYS

The rivers of Europe were its traditional highways. North and west of the Alps in particular, most of the urban and industrial developments had occurred along the main river valleys, while in the east grain and timber were exported down such rivers as the Oder, the Vistula and the Niemen. Here the great change came from the 1830s with the advent of the steamboat, which permitted massive and economic upstream traffic also. By 1840 the trade of Paris by water amounted to two million tons and made the city the largest French port. Seven river steamship companies were successfully set up in Prussia between 1828 and 1850. The entire river steam-powered capacity for all the major German states was then 24 boats (totalling 5,500 tons), while Sweden owned 61 steam vessels (15,200 tons) and Belgium, in 1852, had 364 steamboats.

The economic utility of rivers was limited, however, not merely by their fixed location, which might not suit certain traffic, but frequently also by the incrustation of tolls, privileges and restrictions imposed on the users. It was one of the benefits of the French Revolution carried by Napoleon across half Europe that even after his exile the Congress of Vienna felt constrained to uphold the principle of free navigation on international rivers. On the Rhine, then the river of the greatest economic significance, the principle of freedom enforced by Napoleon was adopted at once, but it did little to help traffic, since it was coupled with the continued limitation of loading and unloading to a few tightly controlled staple places, such as Cologne and Mainz. Meanwhile, the Dutch went on levying their own tolls on all the mouths of the river. Only in 1831 did the difficulties of the Dutch over the Belgian secession, and the growing power of Prussia, give the Prussians the chance to conclude a treaty which enforced complete freedom of navigation to the sea, while it also ended the staple rights

22 A handkerchief printed at Mulhouse, Alsace, with a design commemorating the appearance of steamboats on the Rhine in 1832.

of Cologne. The immediate result was not only to allow the export of building timber, grain, coal and wine downstream, but also to open central Europe further to the penetration of British manufacturers, particularly to the free-trade city of Frankfurt, and it made the British less anxious to support the Middle German Union against Prussia's Zollverein. In the long run the tables were turned, and the Rhine became one of the main export routes for the powerhouse of German industry situated along it. Navigational tolls were finally ended for the Scheldt in 1863 and for the Rhine in 1868 by international agreement. The abolition of tolls and political obstruction in the Elbe proceeded in step with the extension of the Zollverein, first within the Prussian enclaves and later on the Lower Elbe. For the Danube, the other main international river, the principle of freedom of navigation was reaffirmed in the Treaty of Paris of 1856, and inter-

23 Two new means of transport side by side: the Rhône–Danube canal and the railway at Erlangen, 1845. ▶

national regulations for the traffic were agreed in 1857 and 1883. The agreements were followed by great efforts on the part of the governments of Austria and of Hungary to improve the navigation of the river and reduce the damage caused by flooding.

The comparative backwardness of Germany, and the corresponding speed of her development in the second half of the century, is illustrated by the fact that only in 1831 was *Gewerbefreiheit*, the freedom of anyone to enter the trade, granted in respect of Rhine shippers, and as late as 1848 the Rhine shippers presented to the National Assembly in Frankfurt a remarkable series of demands which included: the abolition, for ever, of all large and joint-stock shipping companies; a ban on iron barges; a ban on freight-carrying steamers; the nationalization of steam-tugs and their restriction to periods when either there were no horses available or the bridle-paths were flooded; a ban on steam-tug owners, on merchants, and on mining companies shipping ores, from engaging in Rhine shipping; a return to the shippers' gild with tight rules of entry drawn up by itself; compulsory use of pilots; strong representation of shippers on the Rhine Commission; and the abolition of all tolls and dues. Yet by the end of the century the Rhine ports of Ruhrort-Duisburg handled a traffic (i.e. arrivals plus departures) of nearly twenty million tons a year, Mannheim five million, Ludwigshafen nearly two million, and Mainz and Düsseldorf a million each. By that time, moreover, the average barge on the Rhine had a capacity of 340 tons, and the largest 2,340 tons, and a total of fifty million tons of goods was transported on average journeys of nearly 200 miles on German river and canal navigations.

Much of the European canal-building programme had as its object the internal development of individual cities and districts. This was true of the major ship-canals of Amsterdam (1825), Berlin–Spandau (1849–58), Rotterdam (1872) or the Manchester Ship Canal (1894). It also largely applied to the canals linking such rivers as the Loire and the Seine, the Saône and the Meuse, the Main and the Upper Danube,

or the Ruhr and the Ems and the North Sea. The last link between the Rhine and the Weser was completed in 1914. In Russia, the Upper Volga Waterway (1709) and the Tikhvin Waterway (1811) were joined by the Mariinsk system, completed in 1852, to add another water link between the Volga and the Baltic. But others were used mainly to facilitate international trade: among these must be counted the Kiel Canal of 1895, though it also had strategic significance, the Rhine–Marne Canal, built 1838–53 and widened in 1888–96, and the Rhine–Rhône Canal, completed in 1834.

The pervasiveness of the network of European waterways at the end of the period can be seen at a glance. The network consisted of the rivers running broadly parallel towards the sea being linked by lateral canals, many of them capable of carrying vessels with cargoes of up to 600 tons. There was thus in effect a single system, north of the Alps, running anti-clockwise from the Danube to the Weser. There was also a second system, extending eastward from the Elbe, but between the two there remained a gap, formed partly by the watershed of the Carpathians, but partly by a narrow strip of the North German plain which it would have been easy technically to bridge. The gap showed that while waterways could easily break through the artificial barriers of frontiers, they found it much harder to break the real barrier between industrial and agrarian Germany. For in the 'battle of the canals' which came to a head over the Mittelland Canal project of 1899, the eastern agrarians succeeded in defying logic, the economic interests of the whole of the rest of Germany, and even the Kaiser himself, to prevent the building of a canal bridging the gap, as they were afraid that it would help foreign grain more than their own, that it might open the east to the liberalizing influence of western ideas and consumer goods, and might reduce the subsidy they drew from the rest of the community. The *Junkers* forced the abandonment of the project and the canal was not opened until 1938, when conditions had greatly changed.

RAILWAYS

Important though the navigable waterways were in the economic integration of Europe, a much more crucial part was played by the railway. The first commercial line open to the public, from Manchester to Liverpool, was completed in 1830, or in other words towards the end of the Industrial Revolution in Britain. But on the Continent, railways were part of it, or initiated it, or in some cases could even have

LE CHEMIN DE FER.

JOURNAL DES VOYAGEURS.

Journal paraît le Diman-
, Il se vend dans toutes
tations du chemin de fer.
s'abonne chez A. Decq, 9,
de la Madelaine, à Bruxel-
et chez tous les libraires
a Belgique.

Prix du numéro, 15 centime
Abont par trimestre, 2 fran
sans envoi par la poste.
Prix d'insertion des Anno
ces, 15 centimes par lign
—
Les lettres et réclamatio
doivent être affranchies.

Toutes les observations concernant le Chemin de Fer sont accueillies au bureau du Journal.

24 The railways called forth their own literature; this heading for the first number of a Belgian journal appeared in 1841.

been said to precede it. For while industrialization was widely spaced over a long period, railways began to be built on the Continent almost as soon as in Britain, and they thus struck the different economies at very different stages of their development.

Although some European railways were built with strategic considerations in mind, like the Russian line to Warsaw and the western frontier, most had economic motivation. As the first short stretches of line were linked up into larger networks, it lay in the nature and the logic of their operation to reach out very quickly beyond purely local interests and demands in the drive to become part of as wide a market, and within reach of as many terminals, as possible. The very first continental system to be completed, the Belgian state system voted in 1834 and fully open to traffic in 1844, was in the form of a cross intersecting at Malines, in which the north–south arms linked with France and Holland, and the east–west arms linked with Germany and the Channel at Ostend, connected with the sea route to Britain. While also serving the needs of Belgian industry and passenger traffic, it emphasized the role of Belgium as one of the crossroads of Europe, and there is no doubt that the railways contributed to the rapid expansion of Belgian foreign trade in that period, and to the country's role as supplier of iron, railway equipment and machinery to the rest of Europe.

43

France and Germany were slower to develop complete networks, though in both countries there were some early lines developed on private initiative. In France the first major horse-drawn railway was authorized in 1823, running from St Etienne to Andrézieux. Another line between Lyons and St Etienne, built in 1826–32, carried the first locomotive in 1832. A third line connecting the first with Roanne was opened in 1834. The short-distance Paris–St Germain line was sanctioned in 1835 and completed as far as Le Pecq by 1837, but the encouraging effects of its high returns were counteracted by the poor profits of the two rival suburban lines to Versailles, built soon after. The first major line, Paris–Rouen, was built in 1839–41 mainly by British capital and initiative. The other major line of that period, significantly financed from Alsatian and Swiss sources, ran from Strasbourg to Basle with a branch from Mulhouse to Tann. In Germany the short Nuremberg–Fürth line was opened in 1835 in Bavaria, the equally short Berlin–Potsdam line in 1838 in Prussia, and the first major line in Saxony, Leipzig–Dresden, in 1839.

In the event, the German network was quicker to develop than the French, providing an accurate reflection of their respective speed of industrialization: by 1843 some 500 miles were open in Prussia, and under 400 miles in the whole of France. Although France had by 1842

25 Two early forms of railway transport: a goods train and a cattle train on the Liverpool and Manchester Railway, 1831.

26 Below, a Paris–Nancy goods and cattle train, *c.* 1850, and some of the problems encountered by railway passengers in France in the early days.

Est ce que nous allons, chez nous, dis, mère? je veux encore aller en chemin de fer, moi!!

Il cherche Jud.

C'est une horreur ces maudits facteurs abiment tous les bagages.

Dieu ce facteur qui laisse tomber mon panier mes porcelaines seront toutes brisées.

decided on her 'organic' law, laying down the main principles of building her first network, the rate of building proved to be much faster in the states of Germany. By 1850 the German mileage open was nearly double the French, and despite the prodigious efforts of railway-building in France in 1852–57 (when the 1842 plan was fully carried out) and again under the Freycinet general transport plan of 1878, Germany kept her lead throughout the period. Comparative statistics are shown in the table below:

	Railway mileage in operation in		
	1840	*1870*	*1900*
World	4,800	130,400	491,000
Europe	1,900	65,200	176,200
United Kingdom	1,500	15,500	21,900
France	300	9,700	23,800
Germany	—	12,300	31,700
Austria	—	3,800	11,900
Russia	—	6,700	32,600
Italy	—	3,800	9,700

Although most southern German governments decided from the beginning to build state lines, and the Prussian government, after some initial hesitation, decided in 1847 to follow in that direction, the German railways, once they had been extended beyond the purely local basis, formed a network which made sense in all-German terms, rather than in terms of the individual sovereign states, and thus contributed to the powerful drive towards German unification. Even by 1850 there were continuous lines from Munich to the Saxon system; along the Rhine from Basle to Mainz; and there was the great network radiating outward from Berlin, to Hamburg, to Magdeburg–Hanover–Düsseldorf and the lower Rhine, to Halle–Weimar–Cassel, to Saxony, to Frankfurt-on-Oder–Silesia–Cracow or Teschen, and to Stettin in the north. Only the eastern line, through the agrarian provinces to Danzig and Königsberg, was still unbuilt. Although Prussia from time to time used the railways, as she used all other means at her disposal, to put pressure on other states to join her Customs Union, the significance of the developing network lay above all in its ability to cross frontiers where difficulties of terrain, or a backward road system had hitherto inhibited trade, such as the frontiers with Austria, Bohemia or Poland.

The French plan of 1842, as well as the later ones based on it, envisaged a system in which the main lines radiated outwards from

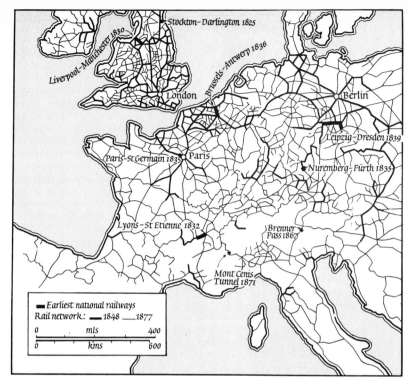

27 Railway systems in Europe to 1877: the arteries of the system on the Continent followed its natural configuration, with little regard for frontiers

Paris, while there was also a major artery linking the Atlantic coast to the Mediterranean in the south. This had relevance to French need; but it also fitted the French system easily into a European one, as the northern line linked with the Channel coast and Belgium, the eastern with Germany, the Paris–Lyons–Marseilles system with Switzerland and Italy, and the Paris–Orleans–Bordeaux line was ultimately extended into Spain.

Railway-building in Belgium, in much of France and in western Germany had much in common with building in Britain: the lines were laid between large, densely settled communities which could provide sufficient traffic to make them pay. Moreover, though each of these areas required some aid and stimulus of foreign capital in the early stages, they were each sufficiently well advanced technically, and had accumulated capital to finance and equip the bulk of their railways out of their own resources. This was not the case in Prussia

47

28 The opening of a railway line in Russia, *c.* 1857.

east of the Elbe or in Austria, and still less so in peripheral Europe, Russia, the Balkans or Spain. There the technical bases did not yet exist: no developed iron industry, no engineering facilities, no management skill and, above all, no capital resources to sustain the massive investments represented by railway-building. Moreover, the likely traffic to be carried, apart from the chief cities and the handful of trading and industrial centres, was likely to be inadequate for the time being to make the lines profitable.

Thus, owing to the lag, or, as it has come to be known, the effect of 'backwardness' arising from the fact that railways spread almost simultaneously in countries at very different stages of development, the actual economic role of the railways differed in the periphery from its role in the industrialized core. For one thing, fewer railways were built, and the railway map of Europe in, say, 1870 or 1913 may be used as an accurate guide to the relative industrialization of different regions of Europe, from the dense networks of Belgium, northern France or the Ruhr to the emptiness of Russia. But, more significantly, because the railways were built mainly by foreign capital, they tended, instead of strengthening the home economy, to subject it more than before to the advanced economies by the need to find regular interest remittances; instead of calling forth iron and engineering industries, as in France and Belgium, their building brought the competition of foreign iron or machines closer to home; and instead of helping to develop a complex industrial economy, the railways, rather as they had done in, say, East Anglia or the Central Massif in France, confirmed the subordinate existence of a single-product supply area, merely encouraging the export of still more iron ore from Sweden, rye from East Prussia or wheat from the Ukraine.

To be sure, in the larger peripheral countries the 'colonial' needs were modified by the needs of the home country: thus in Russia the first major line was from Moscow to St Petersburg, but even there the southbound trains in the early years carried English coal to Moscow, as otherwise there was no freight to ballast the trains that had brought central Russian produce to St Petersburg and for export from the Baltic. In Austria, the first two main lines, Vienna–Galicia (1836–37) and Vienna–Raab and Gloggnitz granted in 1839, had mainly internal significance. But the plan adopted in 1841 for the first state system was intended to strengthen international links, the initial two trunk lines running from Vienna via Prague to the Saxon border, and to Trieste, Austria's main port, respectively.

Ultimately, the peripheral economy would develop also. Whereas in 1836–65, seven-eighths of the iron used in Russian rails and on railway bridges, three-fifths of the locomotives and two-thirds of the freight-cars were imported, by the 1890s the Russian iron capacity (though not yet the steel capacity) had greatly increased, and of the 5,196 engines delivered to the Russian railways in that decade, only 826 were imported. By then the Russian network was expanding faster than any other in Europe. And while much of the railway network existed to bring grain to Odessa or oil to Batum for export, the Trans-Siberian Railway, completed in 1904, opened up a new peripheral area to what was now increasingly becoming a metropolitan centre of Russia: apart from grain and butter, by 1911 one-half of the meat consumed in Moscow and St Petersburg came by rail from Siberia. Thus, though it tended for a time to work in reverse, the effects of railway-building were as powerful in the periphery as in the centre in pulling each country into an integrated European economy.

The logic of railway-working tended powerfully in the same direction. The growing skill of engineers crossed one traditional   49

29 The line that spanned two continents: building the Trans-Siberian Railway (begun in 1891).

barrier after another: south of Vienna, the Semmering line (1848–54) became the first high-level railway into the Alps. The historic Brenner Pass linking Austria and Italy was conquered in 1864–67. The Swiss Alps were pierced by tunnels: Mont Cenis (1857–71) provided a link from France to Italy; the St Gotthard (1872–82) between Germany and Italy; and, the first to use electric traction, the line through the Simplon Tunnel was built in 1898–1906. Meanwhile, the Tauern and Karawanken ranges were breached by the Salzburg–Trieste line in 1909.

Railwaymen were forced to think in international terms and to speak to each other in an international language. Apart from Russia and Spain, they used the same gauge, adopted from Stephenson's colliery railway, and they drove on the left. They adjusted signals, brakes, timetables to each other. There were through trains between the major cities of France, Belgium, Germany and Austria early on and by 1880 sleeping-cars were introduced on these routes. The great international luxury trains, crossing several frontiers, began in 1888 with the Orient Express which ran from Paris to Constantinople. Others ran from Ostend to Vienna, Calais to Brindisi, Bremen to Genoa, Paris and Berlin to Moscow and St Petersburg, and Paris to

Madrid. Through traffic for goods was slower to develop. It was not until a series of conventions concluded in Berne from 1878 onwards and codified in 1893 that standardized freight, trading and insurance systems were developed, and customs duties on transit traffic abolished. In the 1880s several countries also concluded agreements for the mutual repair and cleaning of freight-cars. By the end of the century it was easier, for both passengers and goods, to cross the Continent than it had been for them often to reach the nearest market-town at its beginning.

The sheer weight of traffic implied by the inter-European trade figures could not have been moved without the railway network, which represented the single most substantial alteration of the earth's surface undertaken by man up to that time. Grain, coal and timber could, if need be, still be economically transported by water, and a proportion was; but Russian grain and poultry, the eggs and dairy produce of Denmark, the fruits of France and Italy, the vegetables of Holland, together with the manufactures of Germany, France and Switzerland found a European market via the railway system. Certain cotton goods that passed through the preliminary processes in England, were sent to Bohemia for their intermediate stages and returned to England for finishing. Special rates, and traffic pools, were developed to attract some of this traffic. In France, in 1913, 618 million ton/kilometres were carried by water, and 2,590 million by rail. In Germany, in 1910, the railways carried 401 million tons of freight, and the waterways, 77 million tons. As they helped to unify Germany and Italy and to hold together the centrifugal Austro-Hungarian monarchy within its frontiers, so railways helped to create a unity in Europe that went beyond the economic aspects of life.

OVERSEAS SHIPPING

If inland transport at the beginning of the period consisted either of merely local links by land or of waterways much obstructed by traditional tolls, prohibitions and restrictions, overseas shipping had always been geared to trade between continents and nations. In 1827–36, the first period for which data exist, two-thirds of the foreign commerce of France went by sea; even Russia's foreign trade by sea was greater than that by land. Portugal and Norway had better communications by sea via Britain than by land with their neighbours. Almost the whole foreign trade of the Italian and Scandinavian states, and of course the whole foreign trade of the United Kingdom, went by sea. 51

BURGEFF GRÜN
BURGEFF EXTRA·CUVÉE
BURGEFF JUBILÄUMS·CUVÉE
IMMERGRÜN

Export nach allen Ländern der Erde

30 European exports
are sent to all parts of
the world: an
advertisement by a
German liqueur
manufacturer, 1905.

To that extent, shipping changed its character less during the century:
in quantitative terms, its changes were just as significant.

Looking back from the viewpoint of 1914, the world's merchant
fleets of 1815 appear pathetically small, slow and insecure. The wooden
sailing-ships which carried the bulk cargoes, not only on the short
routes around Europe, but also on the long-distance routes across
the globe were generally of about 200 tons, seldom larger than 1,000
tons; they were held up by calms, sunk or driven off course by storms,
and confined to their ports over winter. In 1914 a single freighter of
12,000 tons steaming at ten knots could, by its speed, regularity and
reliability, replace the entire real carrying capacity of a medium-
sized maritime nation of the earlier period.

European shipping tonnage was slow to increase in the first half of the nineteenth century. Greater carrying capacity was achieved largely by faster sailings and greater safety, improved seamanship, the abolition of the Navigation Acts and other restrictions and faster turn-around. The great expansion in shipping occurred in the second half of the century, when the tonnage of the world's merchant fleet, which at the time was largely owned in Europe and the USA, increased from 9 million net tons in 1850 to 20 million in 1880 and 34·6 million in 1910. At the same time, improvements in the steam-engine and in the iron and steel hull, and the building of the Suez Canal, the Panama Canal and others, increased the effective carrying capacity of each net ton by a factor of between two and three. Docks and harbours were correspondingly extended, and major new harbours built, as at Le Havre and Trieste. Most of this tonnage was used in the traffic between Europe and the rest of the world, but European coastal trade in the Baltic and the Mediterranean, and trade between Great Britain and the Continent accounted for part of the increase.

There was one further, less obvious factor to increase the efficiency of shipping tonnage: this was the telegraph, supplemented towards the end of the period by radio telegraphy and by the telephone. The first electric telegraphy was developed by Morse in the USA in 1836. The first line, Baltimore–Washington, DC, was completed in 1844 and soon wires were laid along all the railway lines. By 1851 England had been connected with the Continent by cable, and in 1866–76 the world's main deep ocean cables were laid. In 1913 there were 322,000 miles of cable, a distance equal to thirteen times around the equator. Meanwhile the telephone had been patented in 1876 and 1877, and as early as 1891 the first Anglo-French cable linked London and Paris, soon to be followed by lines to Brussels, while other European cities were also connected to each other. By 1906 there were over ten telephones for every thousand population in Germany and Britain, though they were at a lesser density elsewhere. Marconi made his first successful wireless transmission in 1901 and by 1914 all larger ships were equipped with radio. The speed of adoption of these inventions was a reflection of the urgency of the needs which they met. The new means of communication not only speeded business, saved capital and reduced costs, but made news and diplomatic contact almost instantaneous; they brought ordinary people closer together, and made the nations of Europe more conscious of their common culture and their common fate.

31 Bitter criticism of the frauds and losses associated with early banking and joint-stock ventures in France; lithograph by Daumier, 1831.

III THE MOVEMENT OF MEN, IDEAS AND CAPITAL

The transport revolution in Europe facilitated commerce, the moving of goods across frontiers, but it is clear that the 'spread' of industrialization outwards from Britain and then from Belgium, northern France and western Germany, as described in Chapter I, was not simply a matter of moving goods, or even equipment to make goods. What had to be transplanted was a system of new methods of production and employment, new attitudes and new motivations. Above all, what was at stake was a new use of resources by turning them into capital. Here the transmission of the process of industrialization over the Continent was helped immensely by the fact that during this period there prevailed a remarkable freedom to transfer capital across frontiers. Europe, in the nineteenth century, was turned into a single international capital market.

There were antecedents for this in the loans to princes and governments in the eighteenth century. Amsterdam was then a meeting-place for people from many countries who had funds to invest, and rulers whose needs exceeded their tax base. The Dutch lent money even to the British, and in 1760 it was estimated that they held perhaps £20 million in Consols, besides further holdings in Bank of England and East India stocks. The total they held in foreign state debts alone was estimated at 1,500 million livres in 1778. There was also much Swiss capital in London. Powerful governments as well as petty German princes resorted to the money-lenders of the German Free Cities, of Geneva and of London. In 1800 Frankfurt quotations included from sixteen to twenty-six different state obligations.

The French wars greatly enlarged the scope of operations for enterprising bankers. Hostilities and indemnities burdened the exchequers of belligerents beyond their means. Massive subsidies by Britain to her allies, and the maintenance of armies far from home, presented ministers with transfer and exchange problems which they were unable to solve by themselves. Bankers who could help them could make enormous profits in the process. The best placed were those who had international connections. The Rothschilds, for example, began their climb to the pinnacle of financial power in Europe by their good fortune that their princely sponsor, the Elector of Hesse, had large funds to spare in the 1790s (accumulated in part by selling the services of his subjects as soldiers), instead of looking for funds, as were most other potentates. Their London branch was founded in the first instance to administer the Elector's loans and investments there, and before long they had branches of the family and of the firm in Vienna, Paris and, for a while, in Naples, in addition to the headquarters in Frankfurt. Thus they could transfer the income of the Elector, who was temporarily in exile in Prague; they could transmit British funds for Wellington's army in Spain across hostile France; and in 1814–15 they could transfer reparations and occupation payments for the Allies by bills and obligations among associated houses without actually having to move any coins or bullion physically. Others who carried on a thriving business in war and reconstruction loans were the associated firms of Hope (of Scots origin in Amsterdam) and Baring (of German origin in London) and British firms like Parish in Hamburg and Boyd, Ker & Co. in Paris. Much business was also transacted by Jewish firms in German cities, like the Bambergers in Mainz, Heine in Hamburg, Mendelssohn in Berlin, Goldschmidt, Erlanger, Seligman in Frankfurt, Oppenheim in Cologne and Bischoffsheim who moved to Brussels in the 1830s and set up branches in Amsterdam, joining with the Austrian rail magnate Baron Hirsch. Another group was formed by Swiss bankers who moved to Paris, including Laffitte, Greffulhe, Hottinguer, André, Odier, who had Italian links, and Jewish firms like Fould and d'Eichthal. The predominance of the stranger or the heretic, and of men near the frontiers, like Swiss and Alsatians and citizens of the German Free Cities, is very marked, and to these have to be added other groups strongly represented in this kind of banking, like Quakers in England, or Greeks spreading outward from the Levant, in family clans like the Zarifi, Ralli and Vlasto.

All these firms remained private bankers. Therefore, although they might be immensely rich, even they could not raise loans large enough for the modern state out of their own resources. Rather, they used their connections, generally among clients having large funds, to find lenders for governments whose unsupported credit might not be adequate. The banks then stood to gain both by a commission, and by the difference between the discount they had to

32–34 French cartoons dealing with financial speculation: top, the Paris Bourse (stock exchange), 1851, by Gustave Doré; left, '"If this God did not exist he would have to be invented" – Voltaire, ex-capitalist', by Bertall, 1847; above, 'Money is the bridge between nations', cartoon by Bertall, 1847, referring to British investment in French railways in the period, 1844–46.

35–37 Three views of the Rothschilds, the leading house of international financiers. Left, title-page of *Das Haus Rothschild* by I. L. Kober, 1858. Opposite, the redeemer from the east, a German caricature, 1848; and, below, Moritz von Bethmann (head of a rival banking house) and Anselm Meyer Rothschild (founder of the house of Rothschild) as the coachmen of Europe, cartoon by A. E. Schalk, 1850.

allow to the lenders and the discount they imposed on the borrowing governments, which might be as much as 40–50 per cent. They might also gain, as they traditionally had done, on the exchanges. The outstanding firm among them was undoubtedly the Rothschilds, whose rise caught the imagination of Europe. In less than half a century they had been transmuted from the ghetto of Frankfurt into the premier financial power, courted and ennobled by emperors and kings and in a position to determine the diplomacy of empires and the progress of railways, and with them the fortunes of half a dozen major countries.

In the first years of peace, most of their loan business consisted of finding funds in the west and in Germany for such rulers as the king of

Prussia and the Austrian emperor, that is to say for oppressive and restrictionist governments whose people were unable or unwilling to maintain them, and for such purposes as the repression of the democratic risings in Naples and in Spain. (The Laffittes financed the rebels against the Holy Alliance.) It might be held, therefore, that they were instrumental in diverting funds from holders who might have otherwise used them to further economic progress, to borrowers who used them to turn back the clock. Yet within twenty years, by the 1840s, the Rothschilds, in common with other leading bankers, were using the same methods to finance railways and other enterprises vital for the industrialization of Europe.

The contradiction between these two courses may only be apparent. The failure of Napoleon to carry his Code and with it the opportunities for bourgeois progress created by the revolution across Europe had made à counter-revolution inevitable. With reaction dominant in Europe, those who wished to advance and to create, for example, the legal and political preconditions for industrial capitalism had to go to work separately in each country. Europe was therefore bound to look for a period of quiet consolidation, of building up slowly the security of property against autocratic caprice, and preparing for democratic revolutions which would use the popular power of nascent nationalism to help in toppling the dynastic-feudal ruling groups who stood in the way of progress.

At the same time the large loans from Britain (there were thirty-one for seventeen countries) floated between 1818 and 1825 – after which date British investors became wary of loans to governments for a while – and the lesser sums lent to foreign governments by the Swiss and the Dutch allowed more of the limited savings on the Continent to flow into industry and helped indirectly to finance British manufactured exports. This was so in the advanced centres about to industrialize, like France whose *rentes* were held in Britain to the sum of 23 million francs in 1823. In Berlin, on the other hand, Rother's policy of floating government loans abroad in order to encourage home capitalists to invest their money productively failed of its purpose, apparently since it was premature, and led Berliners merely to buy up loan papers of Austria, Holland, Russia, Poland, Norway, Hungary, Italy, Spain and even Mexico.

Be that as it may, it is wrong to assume any ideological commitment on the part of the financiers. Living as they did by circumventing the frontiers, immigrants themselves in a remarkable number of

38 A Cruikshank drawing showing the speculative boom and crisis of 1825; these events coincided with the repeal of the Bubble Act (1720) which had inhibited the formation of joint-stock companies (those named in the drawing include several with overseas objectives).

cases, members of a minority religion – Jews in Germany or Austria, Calvinists in France – they had no prejudices other than, perhaps, a penchant for peace, as shown in 1830–31 when they threw their weight behind the peace moves. They mediated where there was a profit to be made. Over most of the nineteenth century there was a profit to be made in two types of international lending: loans to governments, and the financing of railways and other productive ventures. Towards the end of the century, the two tended to come together in such cases as the Russian government loans which were contracted for the purpose of financing railway-building.

Some of the larger firms made the transition smoothly from one to the other type of lending. The Hope-Barings, having floated the French indemnity loan (on which they were reported to have made £1·5 million profit), turned to South America and other overseas trading finance; the Rothschilds, having raised no less than £12

61

LORD BROUGHAM'S RAILWAY NIGHTMARE.

39, 40 A cartoon of November 1845 showing railway promoters rushing to the Board of Trade in London to submit their plans in time for discussion during the next parliamentary session; so many bills were delivered that the system nearly broke down, as is suggested by another *Punch* cartoon, 1845.

million in London for European governments in the four years 1822–25, became the railway financiers. But the quantities of capital needed grew exponentially, and the old forms of raising it proved inadequate. New methods included the joint-stock company, greatly enlarged in scope, the Banque des Affaires or investment bank for long-term capital, and the large discount houses for short-term capital. By these means, the provision of capital was shifted from the few, select, sources, to the masses; from the quiet of the private banker's parlour to the strident advertising necessary to get the small capitalist and *rentier* to entrust his savings to impersonal agencies that would ultimately use them to create the large public utilities – the railways, docks, waterworks, gasworks – and urban building schemes which could not be financed, like most industry, out of the ploughed-back savings of their owners.

It was undoubtedly the railways which conditioned the smaller saver to this response, and next to Britain it was France where their success was greatest. Substantial loans floated in the 1830s had been proof of the existence of large French savings, and when the French planned their first network in 1842, the railways were no longer a gamble. Profitable lines in Britain and in Belgium, and the early lines in France, most of which had been financed by British capital, had proved their potential earning power.

Even the first Belgian state railway network of 1836–40 had raised capital in London, using the Rothschilds, while later in 1845, when the state trunk lines were built and private capital was encouraged to develop branch lines, eight companies for that purpose were formed in London, and over £6 million was raised there for them. British contractors obtained concessions for 770 kilometres (480 miles) of lines. In Holland the Amsterdam–Emmerich line was largely financed by a group from London in 1851–56. In France British capital participated in or dominated many of the earlier main lines: Paris–Rouen and Rouen–Havre, Mantes–Cherbourg, Amiens–Boulogne and Orleans–Bordeaux. By 1845 several British financiers and contractors (including Dennison; Heywood-Kenyard & Co.; Brassey; and Thomson, Bonar & Co.) were linked with one of the main French banking firms engaged in railway finance, Laffitte. This had itself become part British by association with Edward Blount, a British railway financier who had begun as a director of the London–Southampton line and in the course of extending it across the Channel had become a major investor in continental railways. Among others involved were John Masterman Jr, William Gladstone and the houses of Morrison and Ricardo. In the boom of 1845, at least fifty French lines were put before the London market which undertook to subscribe at least £80 million for them. In the event, in the brief period of British involvement in French railways, between 300 and 550 million francs, or one-third to one-half of the total, spread over forty lines, is estimated to have been owned in Britain. This sum, equivalent to some £15–25 million, should be compared with the world total railway investment of £113·5 million in 1845, of which the United Kingdom share was £64 million.

In the 1850s and 1860s it was France which became the main source of railway capital for Europe, though much British capital was still involved, and even German capital flowed outward to Russia, Denmark, Holland, Austria and Italy, mostly into railway-building. The main vehicle of finance was the French Crédit Mobilier, founded by the Péreire brothers with the assistance of the Foulds in 1852. It had had some forerunners in Laffitte's abortive scheme of 1825 to raise very large sums of money for public use, realized to some extent in his Caisse Générale du Commerce et de l'Industrie of 1837, which had a paid-up capital of 15 million francs and which with the help of interest-bearing bonds issued to the public to several times the volume of its own capital, soon financed industry in France, mining in Belgium, metallurgical works in Germany and sulphur-mines in Sicily. There was also the Société Générale of Belgium, founded in 1822; after independence in 1830 this was, with the help of Rothschild, turned into an active promoter of railways, mines and other large stock enterprises, and of two banks, which in turn supported industry on a kind of unit-trust principle. The Banque de Belgique set up in 1835 with 20 million francs capital (of which Frenchmen held 19 million) followed the same course: in four years it had founded twenty-four industrial and financial enterprises with a total capital of 54 million francs.

There were two basic ideas behind the Crédit Mobilier, both derived from the thinking of the Saint-Simonians. One was to mobilize the masses of small savings for large public works for which capital would not be otherwise available. The other was to provide initiative and enterprise where they were lacking locally, and thus open up territories to industrialization. As soon as enterprises could stand on their own feet and provide their own finance, the Crédit Mobilier would use its resources, as a kind of revolving fund, to start up enterprises elsewhere.

The Crédit Mobilier was not the only provider of industrial capital. Older firms, like the Rothschilds, or new consortia, like the bank set up in 1859 by Thomson, Bonar & Co. (Paris) and Bischoffsheim & Goldschmidt (Brussels, Paris and Frankfurt), or the Banque de Paris et des Pays-Bas linked to the Bambergers of Mainz, formed a world of competing and co-operating groups who drew surplus funds, mainly from France, Britain, Belgium and west Germany, to finance enterprises in a wide spectrum of developing nations and territories.

The earliest enterprises of the Péreire and Rothschild groups were in France, but they quickly spilled over abroad. In 1854 the Crédit Mobilier took over the southern Austrian railway network, the banks behind it, together with mines, ironworks, forests and a locomotive- and machine-works at a cost of 200 million francs. These lines were soon extended into Serbia, Roumania and Silesia. The Rothschilds, in reply, created a finance company, the Creditanstalt, and took over the Lombard–Venetian Railway, the Bavarian Eastern

Railway (jointly with German and Austrian capital) and the Vienna Western Railway, besides the Central Italian Railway; at that time, their Italian lines totalled 1,071 kilometres (665 miles) and their Austrian lines, 791 kilometres (490 miles). The South-Eastern Austrian Railways to Belgrade and Budapest of 1,000 kilometres (620 miles) length then went to a consortium made up of André, the Crédit Mobilier and some Hungarian noblemen. The two giant groups also fought over the lines linking Piedmont, Switzerland and the Rhineland. In Spain the story was similar: between 1855 and 1865 the two main French groups enlarged the existing network from 500 kilometres (310 miles) to 5,000 kilometres (3,105 miles) some 80 per cent of which was French-owned. By 1911 Frenchmen owned 60 per cent of the capital of 11,400 kilometres (7,080 miles) of main-line railways. In Russia a group consisting of the Crédit Mobilier, together with Hope-Baring, Stieglitz, Mendelssohn and d'Eichthal, took over after the Crimean War the concession of the 'Great Russian Railway', some 4,000 kilometres (2,485 miles), estimated to cost over one milliard francs.

In addition to railways, the Crédit Mobilier also supported industrial enterprises and, more significantly, it spawned and its example provided the stimulus for imitations of itself. Thus the old international private banking houses of Haber, Mevissen and Oppenheim received a charter in 1853 for the Darmstädter Bank, a direct copy. Other German banks of that type founded in the 1850s were the Berliner Handels-Gesellschaft and the Allgemeine Deutsche Kreditanstalt (Leipzig). There were altogether fifteen such institutions in Germany. The Austrian copy has been mentioned already, and the Péreires also set up a Spanish Crédit Mobilier to compete with two others of that type in Madrid. A Swiss copy, the Banque Générale Suisse, was founded with British and French capital and supported railways in Holland and Italy, gasworks in Spain and Germany and a gold-mine in Central America before it failed. There were several large banks of this kind founded in England, such as the General Credit and Finance Co. (capital £10 million) and the International Finance Society (capital £3 million), both of 1863. In Sweden the Stockholm Enskilda Bank was founded, and others were founded in Holland. In France there followed the Crédit Industriel (1859), supporting industry in Brussels, railways in Portugal and the Russian loan, the Crédit Lyonnais (1863), a bank with an ambition to open many overseas branches, and the Société Générale (1864), supporting

French and foreign railway-building. The most striking achievement of this type of foreign investment was, without doubt, the Suez Canal, financed almost entirely by Frenchmen despite de Lesseps's attempts to enlist international support.

If it is borne in mind that with the capital came entrepreneurs, managers, engineers, contractors and, at times, thousands of work-men it will be realized that in the 1850s, and more so in the 1860s when the European network grew from 51,500 kilometres (32,000 miles) to 94,900 kilometres (59,000 miles), Europe became one single territory open to railway development. This is clear from the major examples quoted. Others could be given. Thus for the Neapolitan Railway, the Franco-British contractors and financiers, Brassey, Blount and Talabot, were joined by a Spaniard, Don José Salamanco. For the Lombard Railway, under construction in 1858, the Roths-childs bought rails in England and Belgium, then set up a factory in Verona to build rolling-stock. The board of the West Swiss Railway Co. had two British, one Swiss and three French directors. The Rutschuk–Varna Railway was built by the British contractors, Peto, Betts & Co., financed by a Belgian syndicate. Two Englishmen with a concession for a Caucasian railway formed their company in France, sold debentures in Amsterdam and Frankfurt, and bought most of their supplies in Belgium. Towards the end of the period, in 1868, when railway and engineering capacity had spread beyond the 'core' of industrialized Europe, the East Hungarian Railway was awarded to a British-Austrian-Belgian syndicate: its rails came from England, locomotives from Bavaria, passenger coaches from Switzer-land and Hungary, and freight cars from Austria.

Nor were these internationally financed links confined to railways. In 1836–39, Cockerill, the largest integrated metallurgical plant in Europe, was supported by banks in Belgium, Paris, Cologne and Vienna. The owner, a Belgian of British descent, was at the time negotiating to build railways in Russia, engineering works and a woollen mill in Warsaw, and a bridge across the Vistula. Belgium, which had invested over 100 million francs abroad by 1830, became mainly a recipient of foreign cápital in the next few decades, before again turning into a net capital exporter at the end of the century. The main influx of funds came from France for the development of the coal-fields in northern France and Belgium: among the financiers in the 1830s were Laffitte, Mallet and the Lille coal-master, Beaussier, and in the 1840s, Rothschild, Mallet, Hottinguer and d'Eichthal.

41 An example of foreign investment and enterprise; the factory of the Franco-Belgian company Vieille Montagne at Oberhausen, Germany, 1852.

About the middle of the century, a great deal of French capital, technical know-how and enterprise went into non-ferrous metals in Germany: it was a classic case of developing the under-used resources of a relatively backward area which then grows and quickly takes over these resources itself. In zinc-mining and smelting, the Franco-Belgian Société de la vieille montagne, founded in 1837, moved into Germany in 1853 and soon dominated the European output; the Stolberg Co. was taken over in 1852 by Koechlin (of the Alsatian banking company) and Oppenheim, to become Europe's largest zinc-mining company. French capital was also to be found in other German zinc companies and in lead, copper and glass-making plants. More important for Germany's future development were her coal and iron resources. Here the leading foreign firm was the Phoenix Mining and Metallurgical Co., originally a Belgian firm turned into a joint-stock company in 1855 by Koechlin and Oppenheim, capitalized at 6 million *Thaler* (22·5 million francs) to take over several properties in Germany and unite twelve blast-furnaces, or one-sixth of the whole Prussian iron capacity, besides coal- and iron-mines. Blount, the Englishman, was chairman and the rest of the board of directors consisted of six Prussians and five Frenchmen. Another ironworks

67

42 Links between banking and railways: 'Monsieur Mercure, associate of a powerful bank', cartoon by Bertall, 1847.

43 Opposite, 'Panic at the Paris Bourse', lithograph by Daumier, 1844.

set up by French capital a little later, the Rheinische Stahlwerke at Meiderich on the Ruhr, had as its chief engineer Gustav Pasteur who pioneered the Gilchrist-Thomas process for Germany. Again, the largest German coal-mining company, the Gelsenkirchner Bergwerks AG, was started by Franco-British capital in 1848–53 and was acquired by German interests only in 1872, by which time it had a value of 4·2 million *Thaler* (16 million francs). The total share of French capital in German industry in 1870 was no more than 5 per cent and in certain key industries no more than 10 per cent, but it is clear that its significance, in innovation, stimulation and example is underrated if it is evaluated in those terms.

In Belgium, French capital flowed into the mining of non-ferrous metals and coal for supply to France which was short of both. In 1852 French capitalists owned wholly or partly twenty-two out of the forty joint-stock companies in Belgian coal-mining. In the Sardinian kingdom, French capital participated very largely in railway-building in the 1850s and the public debt in the 1860s. French companies also developed mining, public utilities, glass, textile, soap and food-processing industries. Finally, French capital was active in foreign banking, generally copying the French prototypes of either

the Crédit Mobilier or the Crédit Foncier (mortgage bank). Between 1850 and 1880 Frenchmen formed over forty banks abroad with a capital of 1·5 milliard francs, of which two-thirds came from France.

Like all quantities in nineteenth-century Europe, French foreign investment grew exponentially. In 1850 the total was 2 milliard francs. By 1880 the total invested was 16 milliard, of which 15 milliard was still operative and had a market value of 22 milliard, and nine-tenths of this was in Europe (including Turkey). Of the total, one-half was invested in government securities, mainly in Italy, Spain, Austria (where the French share was the third largest next to the German and the Dutch), Russia and Turkey, over one-third went to transport, mainly railways, while only little more than one-eighth went into industry and banking.

In the first half of the century, British capital investment on the Continent was mainly limited to government paper and French and Belgian railways. Long-distance investment could not be expected to flow into smaller, industrial enterprises, except for capital that came out with British entrepreneurs. Thus the proprietors of the three leading French engineering works of the 1820s, some of the most advanced French textile and lace mills, some coal-mines and the leading St Petersburg cotton-spinners bearing names like Wilson, Hubbard, Thornton, Wright and Shaw, had taken British capital out with their expertise and entrepreneurship.

Much of that capital was withdrawn from Europe after 1848, when Britain turned to devoting her main foreign investments to overseas territories, but from the late 1850s the Continent returned to favour. In addition to those named earlier, most British finance houses which now additionally came into prominence were of foreign origin: Frühling & Goschen (Leipzig), Hambro's (Copenhagen), Morgan's (USA). A large part of the securities placed by them were for public loans, including the financing of the French indemnity. There was also renewed interest in public works. By 1864, for example, British investors held two-fifths of the shares of the Great Russian Railway Co. The Imperial Continental Gas Co. had thirteen establishments in major cities and an Austrian subsidiary, and several other continental cities were supplied by the English Gas Co. The Union Gas Co., based in Paris but under British management, supplied numerous French cities, besides Genoa, Parma, Modena and Alexandria. There were also investments in mining in Sweden, Italy and Spain, mostly to supply British needs. Such investment bore the character of the more massive British investments overseas in the same period: the creation of complementary supply and market facilities for British industry at that stage. The main contribution of British funds, however, was the provision of short-term credit to sustain trade by the 'bill on London'. Although the French Comptoir d'Escompte and its imitators, including the German Diskontogesellschaft, provided some short-term credit, the largest contribution to international short-term lending and to trade across the frontiers was made in this respect by the London discount market which in its extent and specialization had left continental competitors far behind.

Yet it could not be denied that British investment in this period, c. 1850–75, was only marginal to Europe. Whereas her earlier investments on the Continent had been of key significance as pump-primers or triggers for advanced societies which could develop quickly – allowing repatriation of most of the British capital – the current overseas recipients had no traditional capitalistic basis of their own and would require British ownership and control to stay, thus imparting a new meaning to empire and imperialism. In between these extremes were countries like the USA which could form their own capital but were growing so rapidly that they could use additions from abroad, or the 'peripheral' countries of Europe which had to hold on to British capital much longer than France or the Netherlands earlier on, because the gap was now larger and their preparation less complete. It is mainly to these countries, including Russia, Spain, the Balkans, even Austria and Italy, that some British capital, together with the French, turned in the last quarter of the nineteenth century.

In 1850, it is estimated, British foreign investment in quoted securities (leaving out direct privately held property) amounted to a little over £200 million, of which North and South America had received £100 million, French, Belgian, Dutch and Russian government securities £50 million, Spain and Portugal £35–45 million, French railways £25–30 million and Belgian railways £5 million. By 1875 the total had grown to £1,000 million and by 1914 in the usual exponential manner to £4,000 million. Of this very much larger total Europe's share was still only a little over £200 million, or, to put it another way, the share of British foreign investment held in Europe fell from 66 per cent in 1830 to 55 per cent in 1854, 25 per cent in 1870, 10 per cent in 1900 and 5 per cent in 1914. The total going to Europe was £200 million in 1865–80, only £165 million in 1881–1904, and £167 million in 1905–14. A great deal of British capital in Europe had been repatriated by 1914.

Among the more important interests acquired by the British in this period were ore-mines in Spain, where sixty-four joint-stock companies were set up in the period 1871–1914 for that purpose; Turkish bonds and railways; and large works and public utilities in Russia. Public loans, particularly to Russia, and railway securities still took about half the total.

In spite of the setback of having to find the 5 milliard francs indemnity to Germany in 1873, which was met largely by liquidating foreign holdings, France remained the second most important international lender. Her holdings in 1914 were about half those of the British, though there was also much British, Swiss and German investment in France. There was a parallel shift in French foreign investment too away from Europe, but this was not nearly as drastic as in Britain. Of the much larger total, variously estimated at 45–53 milliard francs, Europe's share fell from 96 per cent in 1851 to 70 per cent in 1881 and 60 per cent in 1914. By the end of the period, nearly half the new French investment was directed to other continents. A larger proportion than in the case of Britain still went into railways

71

44 Cartoon showing France paying her indemnity to Germany (1871–73) by liquidating foreign assets, Berlin 1871.

and government loans, and a growing share of the latter was politically motivated or tied to the purchase of armaments from France. The transfer of the Russian alliance from Germany to France in 1887–94 was followed by a similar transfer of the bulk of Russian government borrowings. French railway capital flowed into Russia, Spain and Italy chiefly. But there were also such industrial investments as the Austrian Alpine Mining Co., set up in 1883 jointly by Austrian and French capital amounting to 75 million francs, there were public utilities, and the wide-ranging investments in Russia. Unlike the British investments, French capital formation abroad was rarely concerned with securing supply needs of the home economy. Investors appeared to be looking for safety and high yield, and were guided by bankers of both the older Haute Banque of Paris and the more popular joint-stock banks, whose advice was not always disinterested.

Germany, arriving later at the 'take-off' point, and engaged in the massive development of her home industry at a time of rapid population growth, was still absorbing foreign capital, on balance, over most of the century, though centres like Frankfurt invested widely in Austria, Holland and even the USA. When, in its last quarter, she had accumulated sufficient capital to begin to export it, her credit balances grew very rapidly, to become the third largest in Europe by 1914. Part of this was balanced and, in a sense financed, by short-term credits from London and Paris. Germany, like France, sent a high proportion of her capital export to Europe. An estimate for 1914 put the position as follows:

	Total foreign investment (£ million)	Investment in Europe (£ million)	(% of total)
United Kingdom	4,000	220	5·5
France	1,850	1,050	56
Germany	1,200	650	54
USA	750	150	20
Other countries	1,900	530	
Total	9,700	2,600	27

In the 1870s and 1880s Germans invested mainly in government paper. Later they also acquired much industrial, utilities and mining capital. German funds were directed towards what were then the developing and peripheral regions of Europe: Austria-Hungary, the Balkans, Italy and Russia, until the latter became politically unacceptable. By 1914 about one-quarter of Germany's European capital was to be found in Austria-Hungary, rather over a quarter in Russia and the Balkans, and rather over a quarter in Turkey, Spain and Portugal; there was also some in France, the Low Countries and even in Britain. With France, in particular, there were widespread exchanges of shares in Lorraine iron, Saar coal and in heavy industry generally. There was also co-operation between German and French banks; and German manufacturers of dye, and chemical and electrical engineering works founded branches in France, and following the commercial treaty with Austria in 1905, others did the same in Austria to get round the tariff. After the crash of 1893 the Germans set up investment banks in Italy. Another expanding German interest lay in the Roumanian oilfield where, in 1905, the Germans were calculated to have invested 92 million francs, compared with 36 million for the other six leading interested nations combined.

Much of this effort derived from the initiative and the resources of the large joint-stock banks, founded or reorganized on the model of the *banques des affaires* in Germany in the early 1870s. But, as in France,

THE FIGHT FOR THE FOOT-PLATE.

British Engine-Driver. "IT'S MY ENGINE, AND I'M GOING TO DRIVE IT!"
Russian Engine-Driver. "NO! IT OUGHT TO BE MINE!—AND IF IT WEREN'T FOR MY LOVE OF PEACE, YOU'D SEE WHAT I'D DO!"
John Chinaman (Station-Master). "ALL LITEE! FIXEE AS YOU LIKEE! ME NO CARE CUSSEE!"

the direction of investment was increasingly dictated by exigencies of diplomacy, and vice versa.

Summing up, it may be seen that there were at least four kinds of foreign investment in this period. One was the purchase of public debt papers of advanced countries whose credit was generally good: this declined in the nineteenth century and by 1914 only insignificant shares of the public debt of advanced countries were held by foreign nationals. The second was investment in the public debt of under-developed countries. This bore great risks and correspondingly very high interest rates and vast promotional profiteering. There were many defaults which, in turn, led to the occupation or colonization of the defaulter and to imperialist rivalry or, where several leading nations were interested, as in the Turkish Empire, to the assumption of administrative power by the agents of the foreign bondholders. It is a moot point whether such loans, to Metternich's Austria, to the Tsar's Russia, to the Khedive of Egypt promoted progress by preserving order and bringing in foreign entrepreneurship, or held it back by financing the subjection and harassment of the nascent national bourgeoisie which thereby was prevented from engineering progress. Thirdly, there were 'trigger' or specialist investments to

45 Opposite, a cartoon from *Punch* showing foreign rivalry for railway concessions in China, 1899; both Britain and Russia were successful.

46 'The New Loan', Hungarian cartoon on the international loan raised by Hungary in 1873, to be repaid at the high rate of interest imposed on loans to governments regarded as unstable.

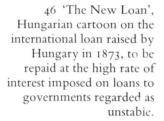

industrialized societies or those ready to accept industrialization; these advanced their progress without impairing their sovereignty, and were in any case soon repaid. And fourthly, there were the massive and sustained investments in the enterprises of more backward economies which did not trigger off native development at once. These might ultimately lead to very slow progress, or they could divert the economy into becoming a specialist and dependent supplier, less capable than before of implanting industrialization. Moreover, they created annual obligations of repayment and loan servicing which could quickly become a heavy burden. Hungary, for example, paid away nearly 10 per cent of her gross domestic product to foreign investors in the years before 1914.

Towards the end of our period peripheral Europe (together with many non-European societies) was the recipient of that class of investment. While it could benefit by the competitive jostling of several mature economies, each willing to direct its capital surplus abroad to welcoming hands, there was also the risk that acceptance of this 'Greek gift' might bring economic dependence and colonial status.

In Russia, the chief recipient of such foreign investment by 1914, the use of foreign capital for industrialization had been elevated to a

75

47 Foreign investment in Russia: advertisement by the Russian-American India Rubber Co. in a St Petersburg banking and trade calendar, 1912.

tenet of high principle under Count Witte in the 1890s, as this alone, he believed, would ensure rapid industrialization without impairment of political independence, without upsetting the balance of payments or the budget, and with the minimum of disturbance to Russia's archaic and obstructive class structure. The largest share of foreign capital was in government paper, and it rose fastest. From a funded debt, before the Crimean War, of 400 million roubles, of which the Dutch held the largest part, the foreign share rose to 30 per cent of the total debt of 5,775 million roubles in 1895 and 48 per cent of 8,811 million roubles in 1914. Only about one-third of this had been used in building railways or other assets which were capable of creating surpluses for loan servicing, but even there the returns consisted in part not of earnings of the real assets but of guarantee payments by the government financed out of taxation. Moreover, since the loans had usually been raised at a heavy discount, the actual rate of interest paid to foreigners was very high. There was also the transfer problem, the problem of finding foreign exchange for bondholders year by year. For the remaining two-thirds of the foreign lending the Russian economy had received no benefit, no assets had been created out of them, and payments of interest to them could be met only by raising ever fresh loans. By 1914 the Germans and Austrians had sold off most of their earlier holdings and 80 per cent of Russian government obligations abroad were held in France, valued at 10·5 milliard francs, and 14 per cent in Britain. No fewer than fifty-two such loans were on the official French lists of quotations, and their holdings were distributed among at least a million Frenchmen.

Foreign capital in private Russian ventures amounted to over 2,000 million roubles, of which the French held over one-third, the British a quarter and the Germans one-fifth. Apart from financing railway lines in the 1860s, before the Russian state stepped in with its support, foreign capital entered mainly from the 1880s onward for the purpose of developing heavy industry, public utilities, mining and textiles, much of it through foreign-controlled banks. The Krivoi Rog iron deposits were opened up by Paulin Talabot and Adolphe Parran in the 1880s. Most of the heavy industry based on Donetz coal and Krivoi Rog iron depended on foreign capital: of seventeen large iron- and steelworks, only one was purely Russian owned. The coal and iron industry in Poland had mainly German capital, but in 1913, concerns with French participation controlled 51 per cent of the south Russian coal output and 78 per cent of her pig-iron output. The textile industry of the St Petersburg and central regions had been created by British capital; Poland depended on German capital and entrepreneurship. Everywhere the foreign-owned mills tended to be the largest and most up-to-date ones. Oil was another area attractive to foreign investors, as it was produced largely for foreign markets. The pioneer and largest group was owned by Nobel Brothers, and the second largest by the Caspian-Black Sea Commercial and Industrial Co., financed by Rothschild. Altogether, there were well over 300 wholly foreign joint-stock companies in Russia in 1900, of which 187 were Belgian, 58 French, 33 German and 25 British.

The Turkish government received its first loan from France in 1854. By 1876, when it suspended debt payments, its debt had spiralled to nearly £200 million, of which it had received about 60 per cent, paying an effective interest rate of 10 per cent for it; only 10 per cent of these funds had been used productively. In 1881 a composition was reached with the foreign creditors under which the nominal debt was scaled down from £T252 million to £T140 million, but a large and growing share of Turkey's tax base was put under foreign supervision to make debt servicing a prior charge, and this included the railway revenue, the Egyptian tribute, the salt and tobacco mono-poly, stamp taxes, tithes, taxes on sheep and cattle, and levies on silk produce and on the fish catch, among others. Under this regime the budget was stabilized and payments to foreign bondholders continued until the Balkan War and the Turkish Revolution brought the finances of the country again into disorder. In the years to 1914 all public works, including docks, railways, irrigation schemes, bridges, urban public utilities and mines, were financed by foreigners, and in the face of the virtual collapse of government power, the Turkish Empire (like Egypt in the 1860s) became a classic arena of intrigue and concession-hunting in which economic, military and diplomatic motives were inextricably mixed. The original influence had been French, and the French held most of the government debt, the railway shares and the shares of the central Banque Impériale Ottomane. German interest was growing from 1880 on, and by 1914 Germans held 20 per cent of the public debt, and a share of the Baghdad railway contract with its important associated concessions. British commer-cial involvement became of significance only in 1910. Total Euro-pean holdings were shared in the percentage ratios: France 60, Germany 25, and Britain 14. Despite the rudimentary industrial base created by foreign capital and the Foreign Debt Administration, which itself had 8,931 employees in March 1912, it is doubtful whether Turkish industrialization was much helped. By 1914 part of the revenue extracted from the poverty-stricken population of Turkey went to pay for a German military mission training the Turkish army, while a French military mission trained the rival Greek army, and British naval missions were helping to build up both Greek and Turkish navies.

This pattern of mixed or rival international lending became typical for the whole of developing Europe. Thus, at the time of the Austrian debt conversion of 1868 of 5 milliard *gulden* nominal, the foreign holdings, amounting to one-half of the total, were distributed in percentages as follows: Netherlands 42, German cities 29, Belgium 15, France 11, Britain 2, Italy and Switzerland 1. But by the end of 1903, of the 10 milliard *kronen* of Austro-Hungarian securities owned abroad, Germany held nearly half, 4,653 million, France held 3,270 million, Holland 647 million, Britain 356 million, and Belgium and Switzerland about 240 million each. The Innsbruck Convention following the First World War, dealing with Austrian state and railway indebtedness alone, calculated the French share as £35 million, the German as £27·6 million and the British as £6·8 million. Similar wide distributions would be found in the Balkan countries, in Italy, Spain and Portugal. Sweden received the highest level of foreign investment per head: by 1913 it stood at 375–400 francs, compared with 185 francs for the USA and 150 francs for Russia, the second largest European borrower. It had risen from 100 million *kronor* in 1860 to 1·5–2 milliard *kronor* (*c.* £100 million), or half the annual national income, by 1913. The bulk of this was German, but there were large contributions from Britain and France. In Sweden, however, as indeed in the other Scandinavian countries where foreign investment was also high, these investments went into developing natural resources and other forms of productive capital, e.g. by financing exports by short-term loans, while budgets were balanced and the population had a long tradition of capitalist enterprise, so that they aided directly in the process of industrialization.

What had developed into a single European market for long-term capital was matched by the growth of a similar single market for short-term lending. This was much more volatile. The bulk of it came from London, but there were also contributions from the older German cities, from Holland and, increasingly, from Paris. Aided by the introduction of the telegraph, the system of transmission of changes in supply or demand for money between the main stock exchanges of Europe became virtually instantaneous in the second half of the century.

The trade cycle, with a financial crisis ending its peak, became a single European phenomenon with the post-war slump of 1815–18 and the crisis of 1825. The crises of 1836–37 and 1839 and in 1847 affected all the advanced centres, including the USA. The crash of 1857 was the first to be truly international in the sense of being felt severely even in the non-industrialized parts of Europe; it was also the first to be associated with massive international capital movements which in turn helped to spread cyclical changes to all the financial centres. The crash of 1866, equally widespread, was the last to be associated with major financial scandal and banking incompetence. From the 1870s the economic unity of Europe and of the advanced world in general was further cemented by the rapid spread of the gold standard, outward from Britain to Germany and the USA by 1873, until in the 1890s it conquered the Russian and Austrian empires too. The gold standard based on the London money market, where sterling was freely exchangeable into gold and where a large part of the world's international transactions were cleared, added another dimension of certainty to the system of international payments. From *c.* 1890 the separate international trading blocs, which had been linked to each other mainly via London, became a single world trade unit.

The effectiveness of investment in real resources across the frontiers was much enhanced throughout by the movement of men bringing their technical expertise, their enterprise and their management skill with them. In broad outline, the migration of leading cadres formed a pattern very similar to that of the migration of capital. As in the case of capital only a few samples can be given here of what was a complex and extensive movement.

At the beginning of the nineteenth century it was mostly British technicians, managers and skilled men who were in demand. The distinction between these categories is hard to draw since, as the opportunity was there, men who went abroad as foremen, trainees or advisers might quickly become partners, proprietors or professional technical experts.

France was particularly welcoming to engineers and ironworkers. Aaron Manby and Daniel Wilson at Charenton founded not only a major engineering works in 1822, but introduced the gas industry to France, pioneered river steamboats and got the major Le Creusot Works going again after it had fallen into decay under French direction. Of their 500–700 workmen, one-half were said to have been British. William Jackson and his brothers at Assailly introduced cast steelmaking into Lorraine and became the founders of a metallurgical enterprise which employed 2,500 workers in the 1850s and pioneered the Bessemer steelmaking method in France as early as 1861. Humphrey Edwards, partner and manager at Périer Brothers' Foundry at Chaillot, became the leading importer and builder of steam-engines in France in 1815–20. Other important steam-engine producers were Steele and Radcliffe in Paris, and in the provinces Waddington Brothers, Thomas, Holland & Stanhope, Hims, Higgs & Co., and Thomas & Pope. Textile machinery-making in Alsace, and the leading French engineering works everywhere, depended on emigrant British skills like those of John Dixon or John Collier, and although the estimate of 15,000 British skilled workers in France is an obvious exaggeration, there were remarkably large numbers involved. Several

48 The Cockerill works at Seraing, Belgium, at night, 1852; lithograph by
E. Toovey, Brussels.

of these British firms included some of the most complete and up-to-
date works in Europe which were hardly exceeded in their ability
to produce the latest design even by the contemporary best in Britain.

Without a doubt, the greatest one of all was William Cockerill
and Sons at Seraing, the main centre for the diffusion of the new
technology across Europe. It had been founded by *émigré* British
craftsmen who reached Belgium via Sweden in 1799. The family
started a woollen mill and engineering works at Verviers, and John
and James Cockerill then set up the Seraing Works in 1817 which
built the first locomotive on the Continent, and produced coke-
smelted iron, machinery, steam-engines and armaments. John and
Charles Cockerill, invited by Beuth to Berlin in 1815, founded a
woollen mill and engineering works there as well as mills in Kottbus,
Guben (where William Cockerill, Jr, remained) and Grünberg. With
every *assortiment* of machinery sold abroad, there came an engineer
from Cockerill's to erect it, to set it going, to train local men to maintain it – and sometimes to stay on himself. After Belgium's independence, the Cockerills received state subsidies, controlled some
sixty establishments, and had a share in the founding of the Banque
de Belgique as well as foreign investments in France and Holland,

81

but the firm collapsed in the crash of 1839. The other major Belgian company, Phoenix, had British managers in D. Bell, followed in 1837 by J. Smith, and several other pioneering machine-building firms also owed their existence to British enterprise and management.

British engineering influence in France reached its height with the building of the early railway network. Stephenson was consulted on the Northern Railway and Locke built the Paris–Rouen and Rouen–Havre lines. Among contractors, Sherwood became a builder of northern lines, and Mackenzie worked to the west and south-west of Paris – Paris–Rouen, Orleans–Bordeaux, Bordeaux–Cette. There were other British contractors for Rouen–Dieppe, Mantes–Caen and Caen–Cherbourg. Some even founded railway works, as Sherwood at Marquise and York at Evreux. Similarly, Stephenson was a consultant for early Belgian lines, and Brassey, Mackenzie, and W. P. Richards & Co., were the contractors. In the absence of any railway engineering skill, the rest of the world, like Britain, had in the early stages to rely on a small handful of men who had laid out and built the first British lines, and who laid down in north-west Europe an extension of the British railway system.

The greatest contractor among them all was Thomas Brassey. Apart from the early French lines already mentioned, in most of which he also participated, he had built by 1870 thirty-four railways on the European continent of upwards of 2,800 miles, in addition to other engineering works, ports, public utilities and bridges and major railways overseas: there was no important European country outside Germany in which he did not build. For the first line, Paris–Rouen, four thousand British miners, masons and navvies were recruited, mainly from the London–Southampton line whose continuation it was intended to be, but in later works only the key personnel were imported, the less skilled work being performed by local men. Similarly, the early companies bought British locomotives and rolling-stock, or had them built locally by British engineers: thus Buddicom and Allcard's works set up in 1843–44 at Rouen was for a time the largest in France. But within a few years locomotives were being built by Frenchmen, and in a short while they began, in turn, to export them to less developed countries, while the British in France and Belgium were repatriated or moved further on.

There were British pioneers also to be found in the leading and innovating works in the other key industries in France, notably in textiles. In the woollen and worsted industry a long line of British innovators reached its zenith with the wool-combing plant of Samuel Cunliffe Lister and Isaac Holden set up near Paris in 1848–49, though by then Heilmann and Schlumberger of Alsace had also made important inventions. Flax-carding and jute-spinning were introduced in France from England. Heywood, of Manchester, became a leading innovator in the Alsace cotton industry; in 1825 some Lancashire printers went to France to train up engravers for calico-printing plants, Englishmen introduced Heathcote's lace bobbinet machine from 1816 on, and in the 1840s McCulloch monopolized the bleaching and finishing of muslins in the Tarare region by methods he brought from Scotland.

'There has been a very great tendency,' averred J. McGregor, Secretary of the Board of Trade, to the Select Committee on Import Duties of 1840, 'for capital and labour to quit this country and settle in other countries. All the cotton factories in the neighbourhood of Vienna, in consequence of the cheapness of provisions, are in a very fair and prosperous condition. But the directors and foremen of those manufactories are chiefly Englishmen and Scotsmen from the cotton factories of Glasgow and Manchester. We find in France that the principal foremen in Rouen, and in the cotton factories, are from Lancashire; you find it in Belgium, in Holland, and in the neighbourhood of Liège.'

This also applied, he went on to say, to the mills of New England. But, he added significantly, while the migrants to Europe returned after 'a few years of profitable effort', those who went to America stayed on permanently.

The more advanced states of Germany, and Prussia in particular, were not far behind France in the employment of British experts. Thus the first Prussian patent for steam shipping was given in 1815 to Barnett Humphrey; after William Wilkinson, it was John Baildon who put up the first coke iron-smelting furnace at the royal works at Gleiwitz and Zabrze, and in the private Hohenlohenhütte in Upper Silesia early in the century, while the earliest steam–engine to drive a Berlin mill and one of the earliest in the city was brought from Britain and set up by the English mechanic Dickson in 1817. One of the most important instruments of the industrialization of Prussia, Beuth's Industrial Institute, obtained many of its technical models from England and America. Jonathan Thornton of Manchester made his fortune building cotton machinery for Hamburg

49 The steelworks at Lendersdorf; painting by C. Schütz, 1838.

and Vienna. Significantly, when Friedrich König invented a steam printing-press in his city of Leipzig, a European centre of printing, he brought it to London in 1810 to get capital to build it. Only when it had been developed and successfully used in England did he return home to set up a manufacturing plant. Like the engineers and engine erectors, the iron blast-furnacemen and puddlers, mainly from the South Wales works, moved about the centres of Europe starting up modern plants. 'That the names of all these workmen are still known,' writes one historian, 'proves how important they were in their time. They migrated to the European continent from factory to factory; most of them were acquainted with each other; many were related and intermarried. In numerous cases they formed groups which worked only as units. We can trace their migration in the same way as we can trace the migration of groups of masons in the architecture of medieval cathedrals.'★ When Rémy at Rasselstein and Wilhelm & Eberhard Hoesch at Lendersdorf introduced puddling into Germany in 1824–25, both employed British puddlers, those of Rémy having been borrowed from Cockerill at Seraing. Fritz Harkort, one of the leading creators of the Industrial Revolution in Germany, employed Mac-Mullen, Lewis and Swift to introduce puddling in his ironworks.

84

★ Fritz Redlich, *History of American Business Leaders*, vol. I (Ann Arbor, Mich., 1940), p. 41

Letters like the following, received by the engineering works of the Prussian Seehandlung in Berlin, Moabit, in March 1842 from the Silesian Laurahütte ironworks, were typical:

'We take the liberty to send you a price list of "Laurahütte" iron, with the respectful request to your engineering works in Moabit to make trials with the above iron, in order to convince yourself that the latter, as also the iron plate, manufactured by English workmen, with English machines and rolled on English rolls, while made from much better raw material than the English iron, will in no way be inferior to the latter. We hope that the prices will also appear acceptable.'

The German dependence on British technology was probably at its height in the early phase of railway-building, as in France and the Low Countries. The first major line, Leipzig–Dresden, was laid out by James Walker, and the first locomotive, its driver and the carriage-builder came from Britain. By 1845, of 487 locomotives in Germany, 237 were British, 57 American, 25 French (from Alsace), 43 Belgian and 125 built in different parts of Germany, mostly in works set up with the help of British engineers. German railway-building required the import of £16 million of railway iron in the period 1835–50. Within a few years, however, German locomotives and engines were to be found on Russian railways, together with men and material from Britain, America, Belgium and France.

Continental entrepreneurs received similarly valuable, and perhaps more durable benefit by their visits and those of their technicians to Britain, and later to France and other leading centres. In fact, few of the leading figures omitted to visit the advanced centres abroad from François de Wendel, the Lorraine ironmaster, J. C. Fischer, the Swiss pioneer of cast-steel making who came several times between 1814 and 1851, and Marc Séguin, the first French locomotive builder, to Krupp, who travelled to England under the name of Schropp.

Other important innovators were Etienne Calla (Paris), Gabriel de Gallois-La Chapelle (St Etienne) and Dufaud (Grossource); among engineers, de Bonnard, Firminy, Dubost, Cabrol, Communeau Coste, Joseph Michel Dutens and Le Play, and others sent by ministries and government departments. Charles Dupin, a leading technical adviser and professor at the Conservatoire des Arts et Métiers, Paris, made six trips to England in 1818–24 and reported on them to his countrymen in six enormous volumes published between

1819 and 1824. Just as there was no major French ironworks without its manager or partner who had spent some time in England, so all the early leading railway engineers had worked with Stephenson or other British engineers, including, besides Séguin and Gallois, such men as Beaunier and Talabot. Among technicians interested in observing progress in textiles were Grandin, Lefebvre-Duruflé and Flavigny, all from Elbeuf, Griolet from Paris and Motte-Bossut from Rouen.

Again, at the end of the Napoleonic Wars the Prussian government dispatched men like Beuth, Schinkel, Eckhart, Krigar (or Krüger), Pertzholdt, Hamann and Oeynhausen to study carefully and report on iron- and steelmaking and engineering, and later there came ironmasters like Jacob Mayer and Schreiber and engineers like Egells, Geisz and Dannenberger. Among railway engineers there were von Decken and von Denis, as well as J. J. Sulzer, the Swiss engine and arms manufacturer. Among textile experts there were Hofmann, Wedding, Goldschmidt, Tappert, Busse and Liepe. From Saxony, visitors to study engineering practice included Brendel, Haubold and Wieck, while experts coming to learn about textile machinery and production included Claus from Chemnitz and Schönherr from

50 The Bell Rock Lighthouse, off the east coast of Scotland; drawings, published in 1824, by Charles Dupin, one of the most prolific propagators of British technology in France.

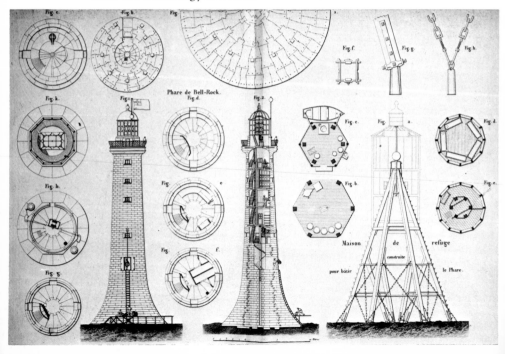

51 Manchester cotton mills, 1826; drawing by the German architect C.F. Schinkel, who visited Britain to study her technical achievements.

Crimmitschau. The Saxon lieutenant of artillery, Carl Wilhelm Bormann, was sent to England in 1827–28 to study coal-mining, iron- and crucible steelmaking, bobbinet-making, woollen- and flax-spinning, calico-printing and finishing, power and dandy looms, and safety locks. He brought back to Saxony all the components of the bobbinet machine, and tried to use the knowledge he had gained for himself by setting up a woollen mill in partnership with the wealthy Baron Lt von Linsinger of Dresden, but they came to grief over their failure to construct adequate machinery.

The Prussian government also appears at times to have had permanent industrial spies planted in England, to observe new developments and help Prussians who came to learn or to purchase machinery. About 1822 or 1823 we hear of Steinhäuser and Eisenwein in London, and in 1832 of one Crook of Liverpool. The Prussian Seehandlung, an official body which acted in part as an investment bank and in part as an industrial trust, picked managers trained in England for its flax-bleaching and finishing works established in 1844–45, and for its modern steam-driven worsted-spinning mill opened in Silesia in 1841. By that time, the export of British yarns and textiles to Europe was managed by a growing colony of foreign merchants in such places as Manchester, Liverpool and Bradford, and there was much coming and going between advanced British industry and the Continent, particularly after 1825 when the prohibition on exporting machinery was relaxed and 1843 when it was repealed. In Manchester the number of German, Dutch and Swiss-German merchant firms rose from 20 in 1815 to 103 in 1850; of French and Italian from 3 to 12; and of other continental firms from nil to 51.

87

In the second half of the century, fewer British experts and entre-preneurs were needed in Europe, and migrant enterprise from Britain found much greater opportunity further overseas. But it was also a period when a few individuals rose to quite exceptional im-portance in Europe. Among them was W. T. Mulvany who came to Germany in 1854, and as proprietor of the Hibernia and Shamrock collieries in the Ruhr became not only a leading coalmaster, but also founded the large Prussian Mining and Ironworks Co. and two employers' associations in the Rhenish-Westphalian industrial belt. He had British partners and engineers, and apart from his sons there were other British entrepreneurs active in important Ruhr collieries and ironworks c. 1850–70. Another striking figure was Ludwig Knoop, born in Bremen and trained at John Bright's mill in Rochdale, who began his career at the age of eighteen as a clerk in the Moscow office of a Manchester yarn-exporting firm in 1839. He developed the business of starting up cotton-mills in Russia with British machines, British engineers and managers and British capital, in which he took a part share. There were eventually 122 such Knoop mills in Russia, including the Krenholm Mill on an island on the Narva, opened in 1860, which in 1896 was reported to be the largest mill in the world under one roof. A third such figure was John Hughes, who developed the Krivoi Rog iron-mines in the 1860s linking them with a coal concession in the Donetz field in 1869 through his New Russian Iron Co., and built up a complex including ironworks, railway plant and railway concessions. He gave his name to the company town of Yusovka (Hughesovka).

Other countries, in turn, sent out their experts to proselytize the underdeveloped centres of Europe. Thus French engineers, metal-lurgists and textile experts moved across Germany, eagerly sought after as technicians and instructors.

'I am enclosing a copy of the agreement with Baclé, and I trust it will be to your satisfaction, since a British or French workman was indispensable for teaching the other men, and particularly for roller turning. According to all the information we have re-ceived, no really first class French workman can be persuaded to leave his fatherland without the assurance of at least 8 francs a day for several years, plus the cost of removal, which is a good deal more than we are paying Baclé.'

This was written in February 1839 by G. H. Ruffer, partner with the Prussian Seehandlung in a Silesian rolling-mill. Other French engineers developed mining of coal and non-ferrous metals, smelting works, and textile technology and design in Germany in the 1840s and 1850s. French managers, technicians and craftsmen played a leading part also in Spain, Italy, Switzerland and Belgium. In the Austrian dominions (outside Italy) there resided 2,500 Frenchmen in 1849, mostly managers, engineers and skilled men, and their numbers were greatly increased with the construction of the Austrian railway network. When it began to operate, the chief engineers as well as many subordinate officials were still French. Similarly, the Great Russian Railway of 1857 employed French engineers, supervisors, book-keepers and craftsmen to train the Russians. In 1886, four years after the British occupation, the Egyptian Civil Service still employed 300 Frenchmen.

Perhaps the single most significant French contribution was made by the stream of graduates of the Ecole Polytechnique and other leading technical colleges in France. Ernest Gouin, graduating in 1836, had studied engineering and locomotive-building in England and subsequently built railways not only in France, but also in Spain, Italy, Holland, Switzerland, Austria-Hungary, Roumania, Russia, Africa and Australia, besides the bridge over the Danube at Budapest and the Moerdyck bridge in Holland. Héron de Villefosse became a great administrator and innovator in Prussian mining, and Louis de Gallois in Austrian mining. Alphonse de Bétancourt rose to be the chief of the Russian Corps of Engineers, and he was followed by Pierre Bazaine who dug the Ladoga Canal, built roads and set up a technical college. De Gaiffier set up a Portuguese body on the model of the French Corps de Ponts et Chaussées, Vautier a similar one in Brazil, and Poirez in the Ottoman Empire. Léon Lalanne, who later became head of the Corps in Paris, had earlier in his career built railways in Spain, Switzerland and Roumania.

Altogether, under the Second Empire, about a hundred members of the Corps de Ponts et Chaussées were given leave at different times to build railways abroad. In 1825–75 the Ecole des Ponts et Chaussées enrolled nearly 300 foreign students, while the Ecole Centrale from its foundation to 1864 had had 4,560 students of whom 1,114 – nearly one-quarter – had come from abroad. But numbers do not tell the full story: it was everywhere the leaders, the innovators, the teachers of others, who were trained in the advanced countries like France. Thus

Heinrich Magnus who had learnt his science in Paris, became Professor, Dean and Rector of the University of Berlin and in 1865 represented Prussia at the Frankfurt conference which officially adopted the metric system in Germany. Many other ex-pupils went to teach at other institutions. Theodore Olivier was asked to set up a Swedish royal technical college. In Austria the metric system was introduced by Jacques Maniel, manager of the Austrian state railways, and later it spread to all the Habsburg dominions. Other French polytechnicians brought the system to Russia, Turkey and Spain.

From early on in the nineteenth century Prussians and Saxons, Bavarians and Austrians had come to France as to England to observe advanced industry actually at work. Even Frenchmen abroad, like Louis Baclé mentioned in the letter quoted above, came back from time to time to keep up to date: on a journey in 1850 Baclé visited works at Stolberg, near Aachen, at St Denis near Paris, in Picardy and in Belgium. In the second half of the century such visits, studies and periods of work abroad became too numerous and too common to be separately charted. Aided by easy means of transport and simpler and non-vexatious passport and visa regulations, the men who had something to contribute to the industrial advance of Europe moved freely across the frontiers to learn, to teach and to build: east European students in German Technische Hochschulen; Italian engineers in the Balkans; German chemists in English works.

Pure science, of course, was fully international and discoveries were debated and developed quickly in several countries as soon as they were made in one. What became particularly notable in this period, however, was the international collaboration, the linked developments, in practical technical discoveries and their application. Thus, the Siemens-Martin steel-smelting process was developed by the collaboration of men from Germany, France and Wales; the motorcar by Lenoir, Hugon and Otto in the 1860s, and Gottlieb Daimler and Karl Friedrich Benz in Germany and France; and oil-prospecting called forth the rapid drill (Germany, 1895), the diamond exploratory drill (Holland and USA, 1905–15), the torsion balance (Hungary, 1890), the seismograph (Germany, 1919), and the rotary hydraulic drill (France, 1846; improved 1919–20).

MIGRATION OF POPULATION

By contrast with the free movement of the innovators and their ideas, mass migration in Europe was of minor significance. The reason for this was that by and large Europe was fairly densely and fairly evenly populated at the beginning of the nineteenth century, compared with the vast rich spaces overseas, so that the main movement, stimulated by the remarkable (and remarkably evenly spread) population growth, was not so much from one point of Europe to another, but outward from Europe.

The European population (including Russia) has been estimated at *c.* 150 million in 1750, 190 million in 1800, 270 million in 1850, and 400 million in 1900. At the same time, annual emigration from Europe (excluding Russia) has been estimated at 113,000 in 1821–50, 270,000 in 1851–80, and 917,000 in 1881–1915, or a total of nearly 44 million in just under a century. In the years 1906–10 the annual average was 1·4 million. It is clear, therefore, that both the population growth and emigration increased over this period not only in absolute terms, but even as a proportion. The causes of the overseas migration of Europeans are complex, and not all of them are to be found in Europe: one must also bear in mind the powers of attraction of North and South America, Australia, New Zealand, South Africa and the North African coastline, and Siberia. The major notable change was the switch from north-western Europe to south-eastern: the north-west furnished virtually 100 per cent of the migrant population in 1821–50, 91 per cent in 1857–80, and less than 43 per cent in 1881–1915.

Migration within Europe across the frontiers was basically of three kinds: migration similar to that overseas into empty lands; migration from rural areas to town and industry; and migration from the poorer, and relatively overpopulated countries to the richer countries, both to their agriculture and their industry.

For migrants of the first kind, only Russia could offer empty land that was there for the taking. Much of the south-east of European Russia and the vast expanse of Asiatic Russia which drew seven million exiles, prisoners and peasants, were filled by Russians from the more densely populated regions, but some settlers came from abroad. In the famine of 1816–17, some 15,000 men, women and children left Baden and Württemberg for Transcaucasia (besides 20,000 who emigrated to the USA), driven by hunger, the loss of civil rights and excessive taxes, and spurred on by the promise of land and a certain religious mysticism which they shared with their patron, Baroness Julie von Krüdener, and with the Tsar. Not all got as far as the other side of the Caucasus, but the commanding general in

Georgia welcomed those who did 'to serve as an example for in-
dustriousness to the native population and instruct the local people
in improvements in agriculture and viticulture'. By 1835 there were
421 colonist villages in ten Russian provinces, containing 288,000
people, and by 1845 the numbers of settlers had grown to 330,000,
mainly in the provinces of Saratov, Bessarabia, Kherson and Taurida.
The growth continued into the second half of the century, by natural
increase as well as immigration, but now migration turned in part
towards the large cities and the Donetz coalfield. There were still
many Prussians and Austrians who came in search of cheap land and
some 15,000 Bohemians settled in Volhynia from 1868 onwards.
By the end of the century, some 900,000 Germans lived in settlements,
and the total German-speaking population was 1·8 million.

According to Russian official statistics which understate the immigration in the earlier years, the annual rate of immigration in
1828–59 was 8,000 as against 1,000 emigrants; in 1860–89 there were
72,000 as against 38,000; and in 1890–1915 there were 69,000 as
against 129,000. It was thus only in the last phase that emigration
exceeded the influx of people. In 1891–1900 about 35,000 left Russia
for the Continent and 50,000 for England, and in 1901–10, the totals
were about 75,000 and 30,000 respectively. Most of these were Jews.
Of the total of 4·15 million people who migrated into Russia, 1·46
million (35·1 per cent) were of German origin and 890,000 (21·4 per
cent) were Austrians; 38·2 per cent were non-Europeans, mainly
Asiatics. For both Germans and Austrians, the peak immigration
periods were 1861–90, when a total of 1·75 million came to Russia and
stayed there.

For Poland the Tsar's policy of attracting immigrants was somewhat different: in place of land, he offered freedom from military
service to immigrants and their sons, and freedom from taxes for six
years, as well as other aids and privileges. The *ukases* (edicts) of 1820,
of 1823 and 1824 were concerned chiefly with attracting immigrants
with industrial skills, and some funds were made available for this
purpose in 1822. The policy was remarkably successful, attracting
particularly German textile workers and others driven out by
unemployment, by military service or wishing to move behind the
Russian tariff barriers to their traditional markets. Estimates of German
immigrants vary from 150,000 in 1824 to 250,000 by 1828, and by
1901 there were 600,000 foreigners in Poland, of whom 82 per cent
were German. Many of them went to farm, but a majority occupied

themselves with industry and trade. Lodz, for example, a textile centre, became almost a German town: it had 190 inhabitants in 1790; 10,000 in 1840; and 315,000 in 1895.

The further west one travelled, the denser the agricultural settlements and the less likelihood, therefore, of attracting migrants in search of land. Yet as there was an even greater shortage of land in the western provinces of Germany, even the settled areas on the fringes of Russia appeared attractive to some. Germans came to the eastern provinces of Prussia, although the social system was hostile to a free peasantry. Between 1824 and 1848 Prussia made a net gain of 770,000 people by immigration, in part to the cities in the west and in part to the land in the east. Over 100,000 Hungarians migrated to Roumania in 1899–1913 (many of them being ethnic Roumanians) and others sought land in Serbia, Bosnia-Herzegovina and Bulgaria. The proposal made by the prominent German nationalist economist, Friedrich List, in his book *The Land System, Dwarf Holdings, and Emigration*, published in 1842, to colonize the Danube basin down to the Black Sea and to Turkey with German peasants suffering from overpopulation, found widespread support in Germany and Austria, and was destined to reappear in a less peaceful guise in the twentieth century.

The second type of migration, from country to town, is a necessary and integral part of industrialization. It is usually found within the frontiers, but even in Britain, Scotsmen crossed the border to find employment in English cities, and the Irish migrated to English and to Scottish towns. The process was repeated in all industrializing countries, from France in the west to Russia in the east, again, mostly within frontiers, but frontiers did not inhibit it. Thus, Alsace, a frontier region industrializing early, attracted workers from Switzerland, Baden and the German Lorraine into the worst-paid and least secure jobs, like the Irish in Britain. Mulhouse alone had 12,000–13,000 such 'floating' population in 1835. In Germany, where dozens of frontiers drew their irrational lines across the living economic links, the movement was clearer still. In the first half of the century, the growing cities and industrial centres of Westphalia and Saxony, as well as Berlin drew upon their natural 'hinterland', some of which was outside their political borders, so that Prussia and Saxony recorded a substantial immigration surplus. Later, particularly after 1890, the trend of the main internal migration was from Prussia east of the Elbe to Berlin or to the Ruhr. In 1907, of 60·4 million Germans, only 31·4 million lived in their place of birth. Of the 29 million who had moved, 8·9 million had moved across provincial or state lines. Thus in Berlin-Brandenburg in 1910 there were 1,983,000 people of east German extraction and in Rhineland-Westphalia there were 810,000. Similarly, the number of Hungarian citizens in Austria rose from 53,000 in 1857 to 324,000 in 1900, mainly in the industrial centres of Vienna and Lower Austria.

This type of migration, from agriculture to industry, may be looked upon as movement from the poorer to the richer sector within an economy and it thus merges into the third, from less developed countries to both industry and agriculture of the more advanced and richer societies. Thus the migration of rural workers east of the Elbe to the Ruhr or to the USA was complemented by the inward migration of Poles and Russians to the *Junker* estates which they had left. This reversed the trend of fifty years earlier, when Germans had settled in Poland. Many Poles, in fact, moved further, and by 1914 there were 350,000–450,000 of them to be found in the Ruhr industries.

Migration to countries offering better wages and conditions became the most typical migration in Europe towards the end of the nineteenth century, as in the twentieth, to the extent that means of transport, and the laws of the receiving country permitted. For example, it was calculated that in 1871 there were 271,000 Italians abroad, 3·6 million in 1901, and 5·8 million in 1911. Up to the 1890s, the main weight of Italian migration was from northern Italy to France and central Europe, and after that from southern Italy, to the USA, Latin America and North Africa. The average annual migration between 1876, when official statistics began, and 1913 was 42,000 to France, 67,000 to Germany and Austria, and 33,000 to Switzerland; a total of 7·56 million emigrated to Europe in 1876–1926, plus 9 million to the Americas and 300,000 to Africa. Most of those who had moved within Europe, however, had come back subsequently. Thus the total Italian population in France in 1911 was estimated at 450,000, and in Germany and Austria at 192,000. The bulk of the migrants went as agricultural or unskilled labourers coming for the harvest or for specific building projects, or they took over the poorer farms in southern France which to them still represented an improvement on their home condition.

There were large numbers of seasonal workers also in Germany. Official statistics show an average of 723,000 foreign seasonal workers in the years before 1914, of whom 404,000 worked in agriculture and

52 'Italian industry has
opened another door for
itself', a German cartoon on
Italian emigration published
on the occasion of the
opening of the Simplon
Tunnel in 1906.

317,000 in industry, mainly in mining. These figures were clearly
incomplete. Moreover, a growing proportion, estimated by 1914 at
up to 250,000, omitted to return to their home countries over the
winter. Among these seasonal migrant workers were 400,000 Poles
mainly for the sugar-beet harvest, and at the outbreak of war in
August 1914 a total of 326,000 of them were trapped in Germany and
not allowed to return until the end of the war. A similar number of
(Russian) Poles were employed in German industry, mainly in Ruhr
mining. There was also a rapid rise of Austrian seasonal workers in
Germany, including many (Austrian) Poles and Ruthenians: in 1907
their number was estimated at 316,000, in 1911 at 358,000 to Prussia
alone (having been only 182,000 in 1905), and in 1914 at 450,000.
About a third of these went into agriculture, the rest into industry.
Of the total of 1·26 million aliens in Germany at the census of 1910,
more than half, 667,000, came from Austria, 138,000 from Russia,
141,000 from Holland, and 104,000 from Italy.

France was the other main recipient of seasonal labour, the totals
by 1914 being upwards of 40,000 Belgians, 20,000 Spaniards and
20,000 Poles. The largest foreign element, however, were the Italians.
Out of a total foreign population of 1·16 million at the 1911 census,

95

419,000 were Italian, 287,000 Belgian, 117,000 German and Austrian and 110,000 Spanish and Portuguese. Finally, the emigration of the Scandinavians, notably the Swedes, should also be mentioned: most of them went to the USA, but an average of 5,000 from Sweden alone moved every year to other countries in Europe.

These mass migrations, like the movements of capital and entrepreneurship described earlier, were a reaction to the coexistence in time of countries at very different stages of economic development when means of communication between them became ever easier. It also worked in the direction of evening out the inequalities. Thus the first type of migration, to the empty acres of Russia and the east, was a form of speeding the development of those backward regions, of turning them into supply sectors of the economy of the advanced regions, and of instituting a dynamic process whereby the marginal product of both the migrant populations and the settled acres was raised. The second and third type of migration reflects the fact that similar population increases occurred in societies at different stages: those which could absorb workers in growing industries, and those which could not and were in danger of falling into a Malthusian trap of overpopulation and starvation. The whole has to be seen within a framework of emigration opportunities overseas, to rich, free and fertile acres, mainly from the agrarian societies under pressure in each phase: north-west Europe in the first half-century, south-east Europe in the second. The striking phenomenon of the mass movement of workers each season which appeared in the years before 1914 is at one and the same time a tribute to the coagulating European economy, using low-paid labour most sensibly in high-wage countries by employing it only at seasons of peak demand – in the harvest – and also a sign of the growing nationalism which had begun to restrict and divert capital movements from their natural channels and was now also beginning to obstruct the easy permanent settlement of alien workers. The frontier which was being made most difficult to cross was that which was rapidly becoming the tangent of areas of the greatest natural economic complementarity: that between the Slav and the German.

It has been maintained from time to time that those migrations of capital, of ideas and of people could not have been of very great significance in the development of Europe, since they never amounted to more than a small fraction of the resources in the receiving country, and were usually temporary at that. However, it all depends on what kind of interrelationship one is looking for. The massive long-term investment and the mass migration providing the bulk of the population that were to be found in areas of recent settlement in Canada, the USA or Australia, were, it is true, absent from Europe, except perhaps for the Russian periphery. But Europe was no empty continent, no backward society when the Industrial Revolution began its inexorable course in Britain. There were human and capital resources in plenty to be fertilized and stimulated. The international stimulation one would expect in such a world would be foreign influence in the earliest stages, in the key sectors, in the progressive and leading firms, which would then be copied and followed by the rest. That is precisely what happened. There was not a single major sector in a single major country or region which was not so stimulated from a more advanced centre, by technicians, entrepreneurs, machines, capital or labour, and sometimes by all of them. Cotton- and woollen-spinning, ironmaking, engineering, railway-building in Belgium and France, mining, textiles, railways and metallurgy in Germany, railways, banking, cotton and iron in Russia . . . the first steps were everywhere led, and often taken, from abroad, together with the know-how and the risks, for a few decisive years at least, until the natives took over.

To be sure, the nature and duration of that influence across the frontiers differed greatly, between early and late industry, between early 'core' industrializers and the later periphery, between phases when only one or two countries were acting as centres of radiation and when a host of competitors had arisen, each eager to spread the light. But everywhere it became increasingly clear that, economically speaking, there existed only a single European community.

Erster Jahrgang.

Zwölftes Heft.

Der Welthandel

Illustrirte

Monatshefte

für

Handel und Industrie,

Länder-

und

Völkerkunde.

Stuttgart

Verlag von Julius Maier.

IV THE OPENING UP OF
THE REST OF THE WORLD

Strictly speaking, this book is about Europe. But the Industrial Revolution is unthinkable in purely European terms. To begin with, there are the United States, where the industrial regions formed a direct counterpart or companion piece to the advanced areas of Europe. More significantly, there were the hitherto empty areas that supplied Europe with food and mineral resources, and there were the traditional societies, above all of Asia, but also of Africa and South America, that provided the markets for Europe's growing industry. Without this wider periphery, Europe might have run into a Malthusian spiral by raising a large industrial population without the full techniques of feeding them on limited land, or it might have fallen into a demand shortage trap before the economies of mass consumption could be launched. For some purposes, it is valid to speak of an 'Atlantic economy', the complementarity of the regions bordering the Atlantic. For our purposes, it is more appropriate to bear in mind the relationships created with the whole overseas world.

This economic relationship between Europe and the rest of the world has sometimes been seen in terms of the 'development' or 'advancement' of the extra-European territories by Europeans. The numbers of emigrants and the quantities of capital exported are bound to impress by their sheer weight. It has been estimated, for example, that in the period 1815–1920 nearly 50 million Europeans emigrated overseas. The numbers of migrants and their descendants living outside Europe in, say, 1914 were of course considerably larger. To these have to be added approximately similar numbers of non-Europeans who were moved, or moved, into the expanding overseas areas as a result of European initiative: black slaves into the USA, Brazil and the West Indies, Indian indentured labour to the West Indies and South Africa, Indian and Chinese labour, free and semi-free, around the edges of the Indian Ocean, or Chinese in California. As for capital exported, the British contribution was £1,000 million in 1850–75, most of it overseas, and in many of the years thereafter the United

53 Title-page of an issue of *Der Welthandel*, a monthly trade journal, published in Stuttgart from 1869; it shows a European factory, a railway scene and an ocean-going vessel, together with scenes of colonial plantations.

54 'Levelling and making out the line', illustration from a pamphlet describing the building of a railway in the Punjab, 1865.

Kingdom invested as much abroad as she did at home. The same ratio applied to France, although in her case a larger share went into Europe. As may be seen from the statistics on p. 73, in 1914 some £6,500 million of European capital was invested outside Europe, 58 per cent of it being British.

It may be accepted that the areas of recent settlement created opportunities for Europeans who could not, as a group, have done so well in their overcrowded home countries, though the indigenous societies, of American Indians or Australian aborigines, suffered grievously in the process. Whether the formerly settled countries could be said to have benefited by their contact with Europe is less easily determined. At any rate, there can be no doubt about the energy and power of a relative handful of Europeans who in one short century in the interest of their search for income and profit overthrew the social framework of China and Japan, India and South-East Asia, the Middle East and Latin America, structures of considerable cohesion and antiquity in many cases. All of them were on an inexorable march towards industrialization, though some took to it quickly, and others were slowed down by being conquered, occupied or divided, or they had their chances reduced by being turned into a vulnerable one-crop supplier, and by being made subject to political decisions by those who did not primarily have their interests at heart.

The interaction has remained complex and continuous. Thus the improved efficiency of colonial farming in such countries as Java, stimulated by the European market, led to a population increase which in due course reduced the acreage available for crops for sale abroad. India's traditional cotton industry was destroyed; but in due course conditions were created for an even larger cotton-textile output based on machinery. Japan turned from a recipient of European capital goods in return for silk and other raw materials, into an industrialized centre which traded with the Chinese mainland on terms of the mother country trading with a colony: exporting manufactures in return for primary produce. The economy of Shanghai, Hong Kong, Buenos Aires or Rio de Janeiro became more integrated with that of Europe-USA than with the economic life of their own hinterland. Even in the recently settled countries, what were originally economies short of capital but rich in natural resources, supplying produce, began to turn into high-capital economies even before 1914, with a large proportion of the population engaged in non-agricultural pursuits and living in large cities.

If the effects of Europe on these areas has been large and visible, so has the influence of these areas on Europe. The growing dependence of Europe on their food supplies, or materials, or markets for capital and manufactured goods, and on space to absorb a part of the population increase, have been noted already. As the world production of ferrous minerals between 1820 and 1910 rose by sixty-five times, and of non-ferrous minerals by a similar ratio, most of the consumption took place in Europe-USA, but a large proportion was raised in the overseas territories. Australian wool allowed European acres to turn to grain; American grain allowed them to turn to meat and dairy produce; the French wine-growing industry, menaced by *Phylloxera*, was saved by planting American stocks resistant to this pest.

What we are concerned with here, however, is the effect of this overseas development specifically on European economic integration. It was the concrete historical background against which it evolved in the nineteenth century. How far was it favourable, and how far disruptive?

Inasmuch as it made European industrialization less painful and helped to maintain its momentum, the existence of the non-European world and its development would by itself have helped to prepare a soil favourable to the creation of a common European economic life. It also allowed the European core areas to develop in greater freedom

and lesser mutual hostility, directing, for example, British capital and enterprise outwards at an early stage instead of forcing it to fight with the French for the then limited investment opportunities of Europe. It provided Europe with certain raw materials at critical times, helping it to avert potentially disruptive crises. Among the most important of these were nitrogenous fertilizers, oil and, above all, gold. The fortunate large finds of the 1840s and 1850s (California and Australia) and again of the 1880s and 1890s (South Africa and Alaska) not only staved off a potential world credit crisis with its deflation and economic stagnation, but permitted, towards the end of the century, a much closer and more productive collaboration of European centres by means of an almost universal gold standard. The gold standard, particularly after 1890, was a very subtle and complex instrument for creating a single world economy, the full effect of which was appreciated only after the world had lost it with the war. Here it is of relevance to note that it rested on two fundamental pillars: the large and fairly inactive gold reserve in Paris which could be drawn on in emergencies by London, where most of the world's payments were made on an astonishingly narrow gold reserve; and the continuous growth of that gold reserve by mining in other continents, particularly in South Africa, so that world trade and out-

55 *Gold Digging at Ararat*; painting by the Australian artist J. Roper, 1854.

56 Packing tea for export in India, *c.* 1895.

put could expand without running up against a shortage of means of payment such as we have become familiar with in more recent times.

European countries formed together with overseas territories an interlocking system of triangular and multilateral trade patterns which could not have survived without all its components and which proved extremely buoyant, in the sense of absorbing potential one-sided increases as they occurred without inhibiting expansion by lack of return sales. Thus continental Europe's deficit with the colonial world was met by her surplus with Britain, which again was in surplus with the colonial world, largely by invisible earnings and returns on earlier investments there. Russia's trading deficits with some countries were periodically covered by capital transfers from others. Purchases of complex machinery by underdeveloped countries from Germany or the USA were financed by capital exports from the United Kingdom. It was, once more, the disruption of this system in the 1920s and 1930s which showed up its value and the fortunate conjunction of circumstances on which it had been built.

The richness of the world's resources that poured into Europe by the end of the nineteenth century helped to convert Europe into a single market for them, all Europe, as it were, standing in a purchaser relationship to the widely scattered and economically poorly organized suppliers, and learning to collaborate rather than drive the price up against itself by disunity. In part, this was merely a question of efficiency, and was exemplified by the international produce exchanges. Tea, timber, metals and other commodities were classified on a standard basis, bought and sold, currently or in futures, without necessarily transporting them, and a single world price obtained which reacted most sensitively to world conditions anywhere. Never before or since have world markets been so free for that kind of commodity. In the case of wheat, for example, it was stated that in January 1905 London received shipments from the American Pacific coast, in February and March from Argentina, in April from Australasia, in May, June and July from India, in July and August from the United States (winter wheat), in September from the United States (spring wheat), in October from Russia and in November from Canada, as the incidence of harvests, prices and transport dictated. Britain in that year had an average two and a half weeks' supply in the ports, three weeks' in the hands of millers and one week's in the hands of bakers, yet there was never any fear of shortage, because there existed a highly organized and dovetailed supply system from overseas. This free organized market for overseas produce, treating Europe as a single area, should be compared with the diffracted and scattered markets for minerals or produce, such as coal or beet sugar, existing in Europe itself.

Against these unifying effects, particularly noticeable towards the end of our period, have to be set the centrifugal forces arising overseas. Even in Europe itself, in spite of a tradition of purely commercial competition, firm versus firm instead of country versus country, the depression of the mid-1870s was followed by rising protective barriers cutting up the European economy into artificial separate components. Overseas, where European trade had battered its way in by war, conquest, guile, repression and occupation, it became clear that as soon as there was more than one European contender for each prize, as soon as the frontiers were staked out and the world began to close in, the latent conflicts could be solved only on political lines, the formal incorporation of territory as conquered territory, as colony.

This phase of modern imperialism began about 1870. Within a remarkably short period of time the whole of Africa and large parts of Asia and some other continents were carved up among the powers, either as colonies or as 'spheres of interest'. Great Britain captured the largest share, adding 4·25 million square miles and 66 million people

57, 58 Advertisements for imported goods: for coffee and tea, Compañia Colonial, Madrid, 1868; below, for tea and rum from China and Brazil, published in Hungary in 1868.

CAFÉS TOSTADOS SIN EVAPORACION

ALMACEN DE TÉS.

COMPAÑIA COLONIAL.

Első pesti ki- és beviteli üzlet

THEA és RHUM

☞ nagyban és kicsinyben ☜

DIETRICH és GOTTSCHLIGG czége alatt

ajánlja a magas s legmagasb nemességnek és a t. közönségnek legnagyobb
thea-rumkészletét a raktárban

„**Peking városához**" és a törzsüzletben „**A theanövényhez**"
vácziutcza 14. sz. Szentkirályiház, kigyótér gr. Teleky ház.

59 'How Lord Roberts wrote Bovril', advertisement linking the meat extract product with a map of the South African campaign, 1900.

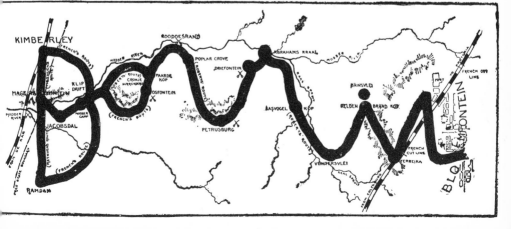

60 'Hold on, John', cartoon on concession hunting in China, published in *Punch*, 1898 (cf. illustration 45).

to her existing vast empire between 1871 and 1900. By 1914 her dependent population numbered 393·5 million, that of Russia 33·2 million, France 55 million, Germany 12·3 million, Japan 19·2 million, and those of the USA, Holland, Belgium, Portugal and Spain, a total of 55 million.

Historians have noted the link between the imperialist ambitions of the chief European industrialized countries, of the USA and Japan, and the armed conflict which broke out in 1914. But while containing a great deal of truth, this view oversimplifies a more complex inter-relationship. In the first place, the transformation of a territory into a colony or an exclusive sphere of interest was, inasmuch as it was directed against anyone, directed less against the interests of other imperial powers than against the interests of the occupied population. In one form or another, by force, peacefully, legally or quasi-legally, citizens of occupying powers obtained ownership or control of their land, their labour and their resources. While this development might ultimately lay the foundation for its own industrialization by creating native capital and modern skilled native labour, it was done without regard to the social costs imposed on the host society, and without an understanding of the social fabric which was being destroyed in the process. The supplies of gold, diamonds, cocoa, coffee or rubber that were being made available as the end-product of colonialization were bound to benefit, directly or indirectly, Europe as a whole. Indeed, quite often the taxed nationals of the colonial powers bore a much greater cost in conquest or administration than they received in benefits by membership of the imperial economy, and might have done better had some other country undertaken the cost of opening up the colony.

Secondly, while colonial ambitions might lead to rivalry, they might also lead to co-operation. The agreement to divide Persia into Russian and British spheres helped ultimately to strengthen the uncertain alliance between those two powers, just as the Boxer Rebellion in China in 1900 brought together all the powers who had been carving up China in a common front against the native population. Moreover, when they turned from promoting them to suppressing them, the European powers found that such issues as slavery or the opium trade formed a common bond in their 'civilizing' mission, and obliged them to avoid the damaging competition that might arise from flouting the general rules in the manner of Leopold II of Belgium's reign of terror in the Congo.

Yet the balance of influence of the overseas scramble for colonies was undoubtedly to exacerbate diplomatic relations in Europe, to realign alliances and ignite hostilities, and to confirm the trend of seeing all latent conflicts and outstanding problems in terms of the nation and the state as the unit. To that extent, the overseas dependencies of the European powers undoubtedly contributed to the causes of the First World War, and with it to the opening of a phase when the movement towards the economic integration of Europe appeared to go into reverse, and to threaten with it the fabric of European society itself.

61 'Wooing the African Venus', cartoon from *Punch* published on the occasion of the granting of the charter to the Imperial British East Africa Company in 1888.

62 General view of the Paris Universal Exhibition, 1867, showing the various national pavilions.

V THE POLITICAL ELEMENT: TREATIES, TARIFFS AND CUSTOMS UNIONS

TARIFFS AND CUSTOMS UNIONS

It is necessary now to retrace our steps and to look at the political dimension as a whole, and its role in the industrialization and integration of the European economy from 1815 onward. In the eighteenth century, state power, guided by theories of mercantilism and cameralism had tended to inhibit commerce by banning or prohibitively taxing imports in order to achieve a positive balance of payments. The search for a gold surplus was exemplified by Friedrich Wilhelm I of Prussia who literally accumulated a war chest of 7 million *Thaler* which he kept in barrels in the cellar of his palace. On the other hand, some governments prohibited exports which might strengthen a rival. Under the revolutionary governments France continued to raise high duties against British imports, and in 1793, when war broke out, she denounced the 1786 Treaty with Britain, excluded many British 'enumerated' goods, and also passed a Navigation Act, on the British model. The tariff was made even harsher under the Directory in 1796, and in the later years of the war, from 1806 on, a mutual blockade sought to destroy all traffic between the British economy and the French continent. It was his failure to enforce his blockade decrees, particularly on Prussia, and the loophole provided by Russia, that largely induced Napoleon to set out on his ill-fated march on Moscow in 1812.

High tariffs were maintained by Britain also, even on grain imports. The Corn Laws of 1815 threatened to wreck the whole European economy by making it impossible for continental countries to pay for their manufactures from Britain. The French tariff of 21 April 1816 included fifty-eight prohibitions of imports and twenty-five of exports and hit particularly the industries of Belgium and Westphalia which had been built up for the French market. French tariff rates were raised in 1820 and 1821 and reached their peak in the Tariff Act of 1826. Austria, which had imposed high tariffs and prohibitions in July 1775 extended them in 1817 to the Tyrol and the new Italian provinces. Russia converted what was a protected system into virtually a prohibitive one in 1810, 1816 and 1821, Poland in 1822 and 1823. Holland, Spain and Portugal had high customs duties, and in the USA protection was fortified in 1812. By contrast, the smaller states of Germany maintained antiquated systems of tolls, excises and transit dues for revenue purposes which had the effect, not of favouring their home industries, if any, but of burdening them, of making all traffic chaotically expensive and of encouraging widespread smuggling. Even in Prussia in 1817 there were still 57 different tariffs left in operation, on 2,775 articles, in the old provinces alone, beside the Saxon system in the Duchy of Saxony, the Swedish system in New Pomerania, and an absence of any system in the Rhineland where the French tariff had been abolished and nothing else put in its place.

Mercantilism was by no means wholly adverse to progress. Towards the end of the eighteenth century it was increasingly directed towards fostering manufactures and furthering the preconditions of industrialization, and this policy was continued after 1815 to merge into more modern forms of state support. Prussia, an outstanding example of a state which in the eighteenth century set up royal factories and metallurgical plants, besides supervising all mines, inviting foreign industrialists, and organizing mortgage banks, and carrying out all manner of other mercantilist policies, turned in the nineteenth century to new methods. Having decided on a relatively low tariff on manufactures, the government then proceeded to assist industrialists in other ways. In the words of Beuth, the chief architect of that system, and a convinced Adam Smithian:

'A state like Prussia which does not grant its manufacturers the import prohibitions or high protective tariffs which would make it unnecessary to care for them otherwise, but which on the contrary exposes them to the cold winds of foreign competition, has, in my view, the duty of acquainting them with the means by which they can emerge victorious from that competition.'

So he became in 1819 director of the reorganized Technical Deputation for Industry, which had the task of spreading knowledge of foreign techniques; in 1821 he founded the Society for the Encouragement of Industry which published information on foreign technology; in the same year he founded the Industrial College; and in 1829 he became director of the Building Academy. Beyond education the state deliberately fostered industry by an extensive road- and waterway-building programme; by freeing the labour market; by subsidies to private industry; by subsidized state enterprises; by exhibitions and prizes; and by an improved patent and joint-stock companies law. Elsewhere the break between the old restrictiveness and the new freedom for capital needed more incisive political changes, but in many capitals there was the same uneasy veering between the 'British', or more liberal, and the 'French', or more controlled approach. Many of the achievements of the French Revolution were carried by the Code Napoléon halfway across Europe: the end of serfdom and of the powers of gilds, freedom to enter any occupation, equality before the law and tax equality, an end to privileges and monopolies, to local tolls, impositions and staple rights, the road open to the talents. It has even been argued that it was no coincidence that apart from Britain and the USA, industrial progress in Europe was limited to the areas *effectively* occupied by Napoleon. Even the spread of the French language across Europe from the noble to the bourgeois classes later helped in the spread of the influence of French technicians. Many of the great gains of Europe, such as the freedom of river navigation, were inaugurated by the French Revolutionary governments in the name of liberty and progress.

Driven forward by nationalism, the French also roused the counter-nationalism of the invaded territories, of Germany, Spain and even Italy. The restoration of 1815 could not quite remove all the bourgeois democratic gains, either of France, or of the anti-French resistance, in spite of the efforts of Metternich. Not many states introduced a true representative government, but any curb of princely caprice was a gain for the security and power of capital. At the same time in the more advanced centres of Europe, under the influence of the economic success of Britain, leading minds made the transition from the Enlightenment to Liberalism, from the quest for the ideal constitution, to the quest for a framework in which advancement would be continuous.

The flame, once kindled, could not be extinguished. European politics, from 1815 to the revolutions of 1830 and 1848, were conducted in terms of demands for and opposition to constitutional government and political 'liberty', which would objectively favour the rise of industrialists, merchants and the professions, and of parallel demands for national liberation from alien rule. As the Holy Alliance opposed all these forms of progress indiscriminately, so their protagonists were driven to press for all of them jointly. The demand for the independent nation state became closely associated with the demand for freedom for capital, even though that might mean impoverishment of the peasant and repression of the worker. Thus was created that fateful bond between the two most powerful drives in nineteenth-century Europe, nationalism and industrialization or economic 'progress'.

The interplay between these two forces, at first in mutual support of each other, while later one became a fetter and obstruction to the other, forms not only the main theme in the European history of the century, but is also far more complex than is often assumed. Nowhere is this complexity more evident than in the creation of the German Zollverein, the Customs Union, out of which arose ultimately the unification of Germany under the leadership of Prussia.

The Prussian Tariff Act of 1818 was mainly designed as a measure of taxation. Its objects were to assimilate the newly gained provinces, to abolish taxes that were inimical to enterprise, and to convert an out-of-date administrative system, badly shaken up during the wars, into a modern and efficient logical machine administering a single customs and currency area of the kind that France, Holland and Britain possessed. Unlike the latter, however, Prussia designed a tariff that was relatively low, raw materials being free, manufactures being admitted at 10 per cent, and only colonial products carrying up to 30 per cent revenue duty. Among the larger nations of Europe, Prussia now had much the most liberal tariff. The reason for this was partly technical, in that the Civil Service at the time considered that prohibitive tariffs would not bring in enough revenue, nor could they prevent the massive smuggling that would occur, and they wanted to encourage transit trade for which Prussia was ideally located. But mainly, the reason was that, fundamentally, Prussia was governed in the interest of a ruling class of cultivating landlords, the *Junkers*, who were export-orientated. 'The West,' Field-Marshal H. von Boyen wrote perceptively to Hardenberg, the Chancellor, in 1819, 'perhaps already oversupplied with manufacturers, sees in England its enemy who has to be fought continuously. The East, against which each year another market is being closed for its corn, longs for English manufactured products and others like them in order to get rid of its corn by these purchases.' The *Junker* class had also ensured that the liberal reforms worked in their favour, particularly the new right of all citizens to buy land. This, the fiery Theodor von Schön wrote to the Freiherr von Altenstein, a leading reformer, in February 1807 in

Königsberg, would raise the price of land, while the sons of *Junkers* could all take commissions in the army. 'Friend! Then we would be made. There is plenty of capital in Prussia. But those who have it happen to be excluded from land-owning . . . I am wholly convinced that with these principles the land will soon be in better shape than it is today. Herr von X. and von Tz. may not have his estate any longer, but on the same estate Mr. W. and Mr. M. will live in a palace and grow wheat where today no pig can find enough to eat . . . The larger part of the nobility will be saved thereby, for their estates will become more valuable than hitherto, and thereby they will either be able to raise more credit or sell for cash, to start on a smaller estate. . . .' Therefore the gains made during the 'wars of liberation' and the Stein and Hardenberg reforms, when an autocratic king had to call on his people for aid, and the interests of the manufacturers in the advanced provinces, were not entirely lost or neglected.

'Our new tax system,' declared the newly founded official gazette, the *Allgemeine Preussische Staatszeitung*, in January 1819, 'is built on freedom of occupation . . . it would be fruitless to revive a moribund gild system which has outlived its age.' It would be supplemented, 'first and foremost, by a high degree of security and freedom of person and property; only where this security and freedom exist does the capitalist have his fatherland'. Secondly, by creating a 'high and noble spirit' among merchants, who would learn to shun dishonesty and intrigue. Thirdly, by 'great national communication works, designed in an overall, long-term view'. Prussia would not 'sell her birthright of a developing commerce for the mess of pottage of river and road tolls, sluice and turnpike charges'. The contrast to be made was not with the protectionist, unitary great powers, whose model was out of reach of Prussia, but with the jumble of particularistic petty states of Germany whose court bureaucracy, in Treitschke's words, were still attached to 'the gild system, the obstructions to settlement and marriage, to the thousand principles of a petty-minded social legislation', and from which Prussia now began to differentiate herself.

The outcry from the rest of the German states over this Tariff Act was immediate, unanimous and deafening. The complaint was not that it was too liberal, but on the contrary, too high for states whose frontiers were too long and whose population too backward, to have any customs control at all. Prussia escaped censure by the German Confederation only because of the tacit support from Metternich who had little interest in tariffs but needed Prussia's aid in suppressing all signs of freedom in Europe. At that stage, only a handful of merchants and manufacturers led by the economist, Friedrich List, protested on the grounds that the new customs barrier, however high or low, went across German soil and not around it. Only a few idealists objected on the grounds that it served to perpetuate particularism, and was likely to delay the ultimate unity of the German nation. Free traders were torn between objecting to the tariff on principle, and seizing on the hope that it might be used to force Germany's neighbours, particularly France, to reduce theirs by mutual concession.

Before long it turned out that the convoluted German frontiers, with their enclaves and detached pieces, designed to weaken Germany, served in fact to strengthen Prussia's position. Enclaves and adjacent detached small pieces of territory were brought into the Prussian customs orbit almost at once; after ten years' experience the rulers of even medium-sized states could see the advantages of a tariff raised at the frontiers while being unable to follow Prussia's example because of the unsuitable configuration of their territories.

Bavaria and Württemberg, both mainly agrarian countries with comparatively liberal laws and an efficient civil service, formed a viable customs union in 1827 and in 1828 Hesse-Darmstadt joined up with Prussia, while a belt of middle states led by industrial Saxony and by free-trade Hanover formed a middle bloc with the mainly negative objective of opposing the other two. It did not prove viable, after an alliance between the Prussian and the Bavarian unions in 1829. When Electoral Hesse joined the Prussian union in 1831 after the revolutions of 1830 which forced several courts to grant more democratic representation and thus become more amenable to economic rather than dynastic considerations, it collapsed. In 1833 most of the middle group joined the other two unions to form the German Customs Union, the Zollverein, which created a continuous internal free-trade area of 18 former states and 23·5 million people, comparable in size with the other leading European powers. One contemporary later recalled the occasion in an oft-quoted account:

... the older generation can still remember how joyfully the opening hour of the year 1834 was welcomed by the trading world. Long trains of waggons stood on the main roads which until then had been obstructed by customs lines. At the stroke of midnight the turnpikes were raised and amid cheers the waggon trains hurried over the frontiers which they could henceforth cross in perfect freedom. Everyone felt that something great had been achieved.'

As its later history was to show, nationalist sentiment played some part in the formation of the Zollverein, yet the more immediate incentives were more mundane. In the case of Prussia they were political, jockeying for position within the German Confederation, and for this she was prepared to pay an economic price. The economic and fiscal advantages she offered were sufficient to outweigh the misgivings of the other contracting states and dynasties. Economically it made overwhelming sense, not merely to create a large single market and to bring together complementary raw materials and industries, but also to harmonize the other social and economic policies of the more backward states with the more advanced policies of such states as the kingdoms of Prussia, Saxony or Bavaria. It was this economic logic which drove most of the remaining states into the Zollverein in the decades to follow, though some, like the Free Cities of Hamburg and Bremen, benefited precisely by remaining outside. The Darmstadt conferences of the Zollverein in the 1830s even seriously discussed its extension to Piedmont, Switzerland, Holland, Denmark, Belgium and, of course, Austria. A generation later, the same economic logic, operating on a larger scale and with more advanced technology, was to begin to favour European integration, but unlike the pan-German example, was to have the weight of national feeling and political power opposed to it.

The Zollverein showed vigorous economic growth almost at once, epitomized by the rapid adoption and expansion of its railway network. While internal trade took an expected upward turn, the external trade figures also grew rapidly, in contrast with the low and stagnating returns for Austria. By 1853, when Austria made its most vigorous effort to join, the Zollverein had by natural increase and further accessions grown to 36 million people.

One of the most obvious advantages of the enlarged unit, which did not fail to impress the rest of Germany, was its power of retaliation and thus of wringing concessions from other states, to end the centuries-old political impotence of Germany. As early as 1824, Prussia had been able to obtain concessions from Britain in a shipping convention, copied later in treaties with Sweden, the Hanse towns, the USA and Brazil. Next, the long-standing grievances of the riparian states

63 Watercolour depicting the first German railway, the Nuremberg–Fürth line, opened in 1835.

were ended by a Rhine agreement with Holland in 1837, followed by a commercial agreement in 1839, though this was denounced in 1841 as too favourable to Holland. There were also treaties by Prussia with Turkey and Greece in 1839–40, with Britain in 1841 and Belgium in 1844, though attempts to come to terms with the high-tariff countries Russia, Austria and France failed. At the same time more and more of the remaining German states either joined the Zollverein, or made treaties with it.

Meanwhile the rest of Europe was also increasingly opened to freer trade. Britain, secure in her commercial and industrial supremacy, dismantled her protectionist barriers and her Navigation Acts between 1842 and 1860. She forced her way into Turkey in 1838, followed by other powers which also obtained 'capitulations' from that weakening empire. In China even more violent methods were used by Britain to gain a trading foothold after three 'opium wars' in 1842 and 1860, again followed by other nations, and an American expedition in 1853 was the first move in the opening up of Japan. Even France had a free-trade party which scored some successes. Tariff negotiations with Britain in 1839–40 and in 1843 were interrupted for purely political reasons only. A proposed customs union with Belgium met stiff opposition from the other powers, but a treaty was concluded in 1842. In the 1850s there were a number of tariff reductions, particularly in 1853 and 1855 on certain key commodities.

The breakthrough in the freeing of European trade, and the beginning of its brief 'liberal interlude', came with the Anglo-French commercial treaty of 1860, a landmark in European history. It ended all prohibitions on French imports and British exports, and greatly reduced the rates of the French import duties. Though meeting much protectionist hostility from French manufacturing interests, only partly silenced by government subsidies to help them tide over the transition years, it was ratified by France partly because of the personal support of Napoleon III, and partly as a method of lessening the tensions between the two countries which had threatened war in 1859. France followed this by treaties with Belgium and Prussia in 1862 (ratified by the Zollverein in 1865), Italy in 1863, Switzerland in 1864, Sweden, Norway, the Hanse towns, Spain and Holland in 1865, Austria in 1866, and Portugal in 1867 and, in turn these were paralleled by a network of other bilateral treaties between European countries, each carrying a 'most-favoured nation' clause, and each tending to push tariffs down rather than up, and to make the raising of barriers increasingly difficult because of its interrelated effects on so many other trading partners. Britain, for example, concluded such treaties with Belgium in 1862, Italy in 1863 and the Zollverein and Austria in 1865. The Zollverein continued even while its members waged war against each other, and it concluded further commercial treaties with Austria and Spain in 1868, and Switzerland, Mexico and Japan in 1869. Meanwhile, not only Great Britain, but also the Zollverein and other customs authorities reduced their remaining duties unilaterally, moving towards complete free trade.

The prosperity and growth in the booms of the mid-1860s and early 1870s, though they were followed in each case by destructive financial crises in the main centres, seemed to confirm the correctness of measures which tended to make Europe a single economic unit. World trade grew by 53 per cent per decade in the period 1840–70. It was in this period also that the leading countries eased trade by safeguarding the rights of aliens; by easing travel; by ratifying treaties on the freedom of inter-navigation; by abolishing the troublesome sound dues on payment in 1857 of a single lump sum to Denmark on behalf of the maritime nations; by extending postal services (discussed further below) patent and trade-mark protection; and by using political treaties to extend commercial freedom to foreign citizens, as in the Treaty of Berlin of 1878 which ordered affairs in the Balkans, and the Treaty of Berlin of 1885 which set up the grotesquely misnamed Congo Free State under King Leopold II of Belgium.

The Zollverein was by no means the only successful extension of an internal free-trade area to the whole territory of a state. In France this had been achieved by the Revolution, in Austria the barriers fell in 1850, in Switzerland in 1848 (completed in 1874), and Sweden and Norway had a customs union from 1874 to 1900. In Denmark, the customs line between Schleswig-Holstein and the rest of the kingdom was abolished in 1853, and Moldavia and Wallachia formed a customs union, under Turkey, in 1847, becoming Roumania in 1878. Next to the Zollverein, however, the most important creation of a free-trade area in Europe out of non-viable small territories, was achieved by the unification of Italy. Here a mass of city states, with their currencies, banks and customs barriers, had hampered trade even between neighbours. Before 1848, freight between Bologna and Lucca stopped at seven toll stations in 125 miles, and between Florence and Milan, at eight stations in 150 miles. The unification of the country under Cavour in 1860 abolished these obstructions and laid the foundation for one of the great industrial nation states of Europe.

So far, national liberation or unification and industrial progress appeared to march hand in hand. Liberation from foreign control and from the remnants of feudalism unleashed everywhere the spirit of enterprise and provided the unprotected and unpropertied labouring masses on which modern industrialized societies could be built up. The ambitions of the modern state, which were to unify its nation and to catch up with Britain, worked in the direction of economic progress.

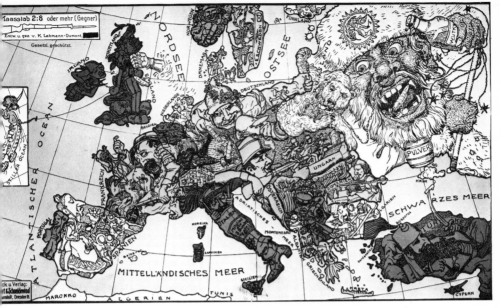

64 A German view of Europe armed to the teeth in 1914; the scale reads
'2:8 or more antagonists', the first figure referring to Germany and her
ally Austria.

By about 1870, however, European society reached the parting of
the ways, though few were aware of it at the time. In one direction,
progress towards the economic integration of the whole of Europe
could continue, trade being freed, and a division of labour developing,
over ever larger areas. In the other direction, the political *raison d'état*
could be allowed to take over completely, continuing the traditional
division of Europe into warring and jealous units, but now equipped
by the new industrialism with ever greater powers of destruction,
and facing each other with increasing bitterness precisely because
attempts at autarchy were violating ever more clearly the economic
logic of Europe and the interests of the people living in it. Which way
would Europe turn?

There was no lack of initiative for supranational customs unions.
In France unofficial attempts were made for such a union with Germany about 1888; the Hungarians attempted a central European
union in 1885–86; but the most persistent attempt, almost continuous
from the 1880s to 1914, was to link Germany with its neighbours in a
variously named 'Central European Economic Association' to include   119

not only Austria-Hungary, Belgium, Holland, Switzerland and Denmark, but at times even countries as far afield as Italy, Roumania and Sweden. None of this was taken seriously by the Cabinets of Europe, except in the distorted form of the expansionist German war aims of 1915–17 to incorporate the Balkans, Turkey and perhaps even the Ukraine into a German-dominated economic empire.

INTERNATIONAL MONETARY AGREEMENTS

More practical than the attempts to form international economic unions were those to follow up the internal unification of currency, weights and measures which had greatly helped the French from the 1790s and the Germans from the 1850s. An international Bureau of Weights and Measures was set up in Paris in 1875 after numerous European countries had adopted the (French) metric system. As far as currency was concerned, the most significant development (apart from the rise of the Sterling Area, which mainly affected areas outside Europe) was the creation of the Latin Monetary Union in 1865. The basis of this union was the French franc, established by Napoleon's Act of 1803 as a metric coin on a bimetallic base. The Belgians, after achieving their independence, based their franc on the French coin in 1832 and so did the Swiss when they reformed their chaotic coinage in 1850. The Italians followed suit, since Piedmont had retained the franc (named the lira) from the days of the French occupation. Following the gold discoveries of the mid-century, the foundations of the French bimetallic franc were severely shaken: in effect, it changed about 1848 from a silver to a gold standard. As French gold moved into the neighbouring countries, Italy and Switzerland reduced the silver in their coinage in the early 1860s while yet leaving their coinage interchangeable, so that these inferior coins flowed in large quantities first into France and then into Belgium. The resulting monetary chaos led to a conference in 1865 which established by treaty the Latin Monetary Union between the four countries, Greece joining in 1867.

Other countries accepting the gold franc (not the bimetallic system) as the basis of their coinage included both Austria and Hungary (1867), Spain and her colonies (1868), Finland (1877), Serbia (1878) and Bulgaria (1880), besides the French colonies and several Latin American countries. Remarkably enough, the Latin Monetary Union survived further violent fluctuations in the price of silver, inflation among some of its members, and even tariff wars between them until the First

World War, though undoubtedly one of the reasons for that tenacity was the fact that no country could have afforded to redeem its coins held by the others. A Scandinavian monetary union, based on the crown of 100 *ore*, was set up in 1873 and 1875 between Sweden, Denmark and Norway.

In the main, however, the efforts of governments tended in the other direction, towards the increasing disruption of the European economy. This was probably inevitable: the new bourgeois nation state, carried forward by the progressive policies it represented in an earlier stage, now by its inner logic turned into a fetter on progress, first by attempting to protect itself against foreign imports and gaining military strength through autarky, and finally by imperialist and militarist adventures necessarily ending in war. In those circumstances the powerful internal pressure groups easily turned to their state for tariff protection and discrimination against foreigners, though the continuing and strengthened international links between capitalist enterprises which went on at the same time showed that this was by no means a necessary or natural course for them to take.

PROTECTIONIST POLICIES

The 'liberal' interlude in Europe lasted barely two decades. The first major breach in it was made by Germany's Tariff Act of 1879, although Austria-Hungary which had never gone far along the free-trade road, had reverted from the more liberal 'treaty' tariff to the more protectionist 'autonomous' tariff with its main trading partners in 1876 and 1878. Italy also raised her tariffs in 1878 and again in 1887,

65 The effect of the Tariff Act of 1879: a cartoon showing the victim, Germany, bound with protective tariffs and financial conflicts (cf. illustration 20).

121

Switzerland in 1884, 1891 and again in 1906, Austria in 1882, and France after moderate rises in 1881, reorganized her protective system by the massive Méline tariff of 1892, which was again raised in 1910. In Germany itself tariff rates for agricultural products continued upwards, though the German manufacturers, seeking low home costs for their expanding exports, persuaded the Caprivi government to lower the operative rates from 1891 on by a series of twelve-year commercial treaties including most-favoured-nation clauses with all the main trading nations. By 1902, however, the agrarians had reversed this trend, and German tariffs went up again. This upward shift of tariffs was also followed by Russia and most of the smaller countries of Europe, as well as by the USA. Only Holland and the United Kingdom preserved their free-trade policies.

The immediate trigger releasing this reversing move was often the impact of the cheap grain which flooded Europe in unprecedented quantities in the late 1870s, but it was reinforced by the impact of the 'Great Depression' in European industry beginning after the collapse of the boom of 1873. As food prices were raised in some countries by means of a tariff, manufacturers had cause to call for protection, partly to compensate them for the raised cost of living of their workers, but partly to safeguard them from the alleged dumping by neighbouring countries. The compact of 'rye and iron' which was behind the German tariff of 1879 was typical of what happened in most countries of Europe. Paradoxically, it was therefore the very success of the great investments of the mid-1860s and early 1870s – which ought to have benefited the European consumer, and in fact did benefit him by lower real costs and prices – which set off the economic disruption of Europe that was to end in a general war. If the impact, of cheaper food in particular, had come more slowly, the agrarian population on the Continent might, like that of Britain, have adjusted to it by migrating to industry, but it came too quickly. Moreover, the agrarians everywhere wielded political power far in excess of their numbers, and wielded it in desperation as they saw it slipping away. On the issue of protection they had willing allies in industrialists unprepared as yet to accept a system of low prices and low profits on a large turnover, and who instead gave the name of 'depression' to a twenty-year period in which standards of living rose faster in western Europe than ever before.

At times, these tariffs, particularly when directed against individual countries, would lead to specific retaliation and to veritable tariff 'wars'. The conflict between France and Switzerland which broke out as a result of the Méline tariff and lasted for two-and-a-half years, 1892–95, greatly reduced trade between these complementary economies, but was mainly economic in nature. It is significant that the other two major tariff wars, though they did much economic damage, both had strong political overtones. The German-Russian conflict of 1893–94 was relatively short, and led to a temporary expansion of trade after its conclusion. The conflict between Italy and France which broke out in 1887 lasted in effect for ten years and had devastating consequences for Italy, for whom France had been the chief market. In its course Frenchmen who had provided much of the capital for the industrialization of Italy sold about half of it, dumping their securities in large quantities on the Italian market. Their hostility was caused in part by the conclusion in 1882 of the alliance between Italy, Germany and Austria.

In addition to tariffs, there were also other measures to favour home capital: shipping bounties and subsidies, particularly in France, railway preferences for German exports and for eastern emigrants using Bremen rather than non-German ports, and a special schedule aiding home industry devised by the Russian railways in 1891–93.

The immediate effect of all these measures is not easy to gauge. Trade continued to increase faster than production throughout the protectionist phase: thus the annual rate of world trade rose by 3·4 per cent while production rose by only 2·1 per cent and a large part of that increase was captured by European countries, particularly Germany. Caprivi's treaties, each with its most-favoured-nation clause, clearly benefited German manufacturers more than any others as they stood poised ready with their efficient modern low-cost capital to take advantage of any available market. Again, the rate at which countries like Germany or Italy became dependent on imported food, in spite of all their expensive protection and subsidies, appeared to differ very little from the rate of Great Britain at a similar stage of development.

INTERNATIONAL ORGANIZATIONS AND CONVENTIONS

It could be argued that while the European governments pursued their normal diplomatic game of the war of each against all, day-by-day forging of closer economic and social links between the peoples of Europe went on regardless. Most of it was natural, arising not out of some ideological inspiration, but out of the needs of people and of   123 businesses and other organizations. Frequently the growing economic interdependence of Europe also expressed itself in the need for an international institution to make the national one perform its work fully.

The Universal Postal Union (UPU) was a good example. Typically, it had been preceded by the creation of a logical and efficient penny post, first in Britain in 1840, and soon after, on the same basis, in Germany. The German example, which replaced a corrupt and chaotic mixture of state and private contractors' systems, showed the possibilities of international collaboration. It started with the working of the Austro-Prussian postal union of 1850 when there were still seventeen separate postal systems in Germany, whereas by 1867 there was in effect only one. An earlier conference of fifteen states in Paris in 1863 had been fruitless, but the potential gains were too great to accept failure, and a successful union was formed in 1874 in Berne by twenty-one states with a population of 350 million. It was clear that it was in the interest of everyone, and to the detriment of no one, to extend a cheap, unified, regular and predictable postal service to as many parts of the world as possible. As late as 1862, a letter from Germany to Rome paid 68 *Pfennigs* via Switzerland by land, 90 *Pf.* via Switzerland, Genoa and then by water, 48 *Pf.* via Austria, and 85 *Pf.* via France, the first franking all the way, the rest to the borders of the Vatican State only. The agreement of 1874 was for a common international letter rate, later also extending to parcels, for lower rates for postcards, samples and printed matter, for registered mail, and, for the sake of simplicity and low costs of operation, for the collection of revenue in the sender country, the receiving country delivering mail free. The main divergent interests, those of countries handling much transit traffic without having much originating in their own borders, were compensated by small transit payments. This Universal Postal Union, as it became in 1878 with the accession of more states, was an extension of the facilities offered by fast, cheap and reliable means of transport and in turn depended on them and their improvement. Letters handled by the UPU increased from 144 million in 1875 to 2,500 million in 1913.

The Postal Union had been preceded, in 1865, by an international telegraph treaty, signed by twenty European states, and by an International Telegraphic Office established in Berne in 1869. In 1883 the Convention of Paris attempted to protect patents and trade marks on an international basis, and the Berne Convention on copyright was

66 Laying cables at Cologne for the underground telegraph system of the German Empire; painting by Christian Sell.

signed in 1886. In 1863 there had been an international agreement to protect submarine telegraphic cables, and in 1906 an International Radiotelegraphic Union took its place beside the older Union.

There were agreements to end piracy, for freedom of the sea, for rules of the road at sea, and in 1879 the London Conference adopted as international code the British code of distress signals. There was a Brussels convention in 1910 on collisions at sea and a London conference on safety in 1914 after the *Titanic* disaster, although international agreement on a load-line was not reached until 1930. A convention for free access for ships of all nations to the Suez Canal came into effective force in 1904; for the Panama Canal it was guaranteed in 1901 and for the Kiel Canal by the Treaty of Versailles of 1919. To railway agreements and agreements on river navigation, noted above, has to be added the International Automobile Convention of 1909 of Paris.

The industrialized world also discovered that public health, like peace, was indivisible. A series of conventions, beginning with one called in 1853 by Napoleon III, proved unable to agree on concerted measures to prevent the spread of epidemics from the Orient, though a number of international medical bureaux were set up and an international sanitary commission established in Egypt in 1881. The first effective international sanitary convention was that of Venice of 1892, uniting the efforts of fourteen countries to stop the import of diseases through the Suez Canal. It was followed quickly by the Dresden Convention (1893) to stamp out cholera in Europe; the Paris Convention (1894) to fight it in its countries of origin; and the Venice Convention (1897) against the plague. The Paris Convention of 1903 unified the agreements on the plague, cholera and yellow fever, and in 1907 an International Office of Public Health was founded.

A meeting held in Shanghai in 1909 by thirteen leading states considered the opium traffic and at The Hague in 1912 several countries agreed to prohibit the trade in opium and dangerous drugs. A General Act of Brussels of 1890 prohibited the sale of liquor and rifles to Africans in certain areas, and in the same year the USA and the leading European powers signed the General Act of the Anti-Slavery Conference in Brussels, to take measures to stamp out the slave-trade: this was a remarkable change, reflecting the transformed economic conditions of what had formerly been the chief slaving and opium-selling nations.

Nearer home, Switzerland was the first in 1881 to propose an international convention to protect labour and, incidentally, to ensure that the exports of the more advanced countries were not undercut by unfair labour practices of the others. In 1890, on the initiative of the Kaiser, a meeting finally took place in Berlin and the representatives of fifteen nations subscribed to some desirable principles, though they were nowhere adopted. It may, however, be claimed that the International Labour Office set up in 1919 obtained some of its inspiration from that meeting. Moreover, the two Berne Conventions of 1906, prohibiting the night employment of women and the manufacture and sale of white phosphorus matches, and the third Labour Conference of Berne of 1913, at which twelve states signed a convention for a maximum ten-hour day for women and children, and another prohibiting night work for children, may be said to have taken their inspiration from the original Berlin meeting. There were bilateral treaties between countries linked by labour migrations, such

126

as France and Belgium in 1882, and France and Italy and France and Switzerland in 1904, to ease the transfer of savings, of insurance claims, etc., for migrant workers.

Another important area of growth was international private law. There were agreements on compensation for collisions at sea, bilateral treaties on extradition of criminals, on the hiring of ships' crews, and the Institut de droit international, 1873. The Hague Conferences of 1893–1904 led to agreements among fifteen leading nations on marriage, divorce, wardship and other private law matters. In the sphere of the laws of war, the conference at Geneva in 1864 settled minimal rules on the treatment of prisoners of war and of the wounded, and this was extended in 1906 and applied to naval warfare by The Hague conferences. In 1899 there were international declarations on land warfare, particularly on dropping explosives from balloons, on the use of poison gas and of dum-dum bullets.

This enumeration barely scratches the surface of the mountain of international conventions, associations and meetings which were called into being by the needs of the day or the desire of citizens in the last half-century before 1914. They ranged from international sugar and fisheries conventions to agreements on the preservation of rare species; from scientific collaboration, as in the International Geodetic Society of 1864 of Potsdam, expanded in 1875 by the Berlin Convention to measure the earth accurately, to international trade exhibitions held by agreement approximately every third year; from an international Rotarians society of 1912 and the Olympic Games since 1896 to the Nobel Peace Prize and the Carnegie Foundation for Peace. One study lists at least four hundred international bodies of this kind by 1914, and another lists eighty-six valid international conventions or official declarations at that date.

These links maintained by governments were reflected, and paralleled, by the organizations of economic life. The cartel and the trust, the new powerful associations of capital, have often been said to have been dependent on protection against foreign competition. In fact, they themselves tended to become increasingly international, to carve up the world as if boundaries did not exist. Among the best known are the international rail cartel of 1883, undoubtedly one of the earliest, the dynamite cartel of 1886, and the international shipping conferences, standardizing freight and passenger rates on the main routes from 1892 onwards. By 1897 there were forty international cartels in which Germans participated, and in 1914 there were at least 114. They were particularly strong in chemicals, in iron and steel, transport and textiles. Others were the British-American tobacco carve-up and the attempt in 1902 by J.P. Morgan's International Mercantile Marine to monopolize the North Atlantic shipping routes.

Another new phenomenon was the international company, either spreading outward from one country to found daughter organizations, like Standard Oil, or combining previously existing firms in different countries into a single unit, like Royal Dutch Shell operating as such since 1907 and the Turkish Petroleum Co. of 1912. These were firms building their international links not so much from considerations of finance, as the earlier banks had done, but for reasons of technical logic and real costs.

The internationalization of capital was followed by that of labour. Some unions, especially those of miners, metalworkers and transport workers, began to forge international links in the 1890s, and in 1903 there was a general federation formed which in 1913, with the accession of the American Federation of Labor, became the International Federation of Trade Unions. The First International of Workingmen lasted from 1864 to 1876. The Second International, founded in 1889, embraced the majority of socialist parties on the Continent which, in turn, had close or even controlling relations with their respective trade union movements. The parties associated in the International considered themselves the true representatives of the working classes of their countries and, where there was no democratic control of government, the true representatives of the people at large. For this reason, and for deeper reasons of ideology, they were opposed to the imperialism, militarism and growth of armaments they saw around them, and took a strong stand against them particularly at the Congresses of Brussels (1891), Paris (1900), Amsterdam (1904), Stuttgart (1907) and Basle (1912). By the famous resolution of the Stuttgart Congress they obliged themselves to use the power of the working classes to prevent the outbreak of a war, and, if it should break out none the less, to work for its speedy end and at the same time to use the resulting crisis to rouse the masses to bring down the rule of their own capitalist class.

These organizations and associations, to be sure, covered areas of the globe outside Europe. But in each case the European states (together generally with the USA) formed much the most important part of the membership and supplied most of the drive, while in most cases the objective was to define the relationship of the states of Europe among themselves. At that time, world economic integration was in no sense antagonistic to European integration which, on the contrary, appeared to be a necessary preliminary part of it.

This is true also of a widespread peace movement, inspired by a variety of motives. Even governments had been persuaded by Tsar Nicholas II, who was conscious that Russia had fallen behind in the arms race, to meet at The Hague Conferences of 1899 and 1907. No fewer than twenty-six were represented at the first, and forty-four at the second, and among other work, they accepted certain restrictions on land warfare (noted above) and the setting up of a Permanent Court of Arbitration between nations. More continuous, and no doubt more sincere, were the efforts of several powerful international peace associations who based themselves, at least in part, on the notion that a major war between the great powers had now become unthinkable and would therefore not take place.

The best-known expression of this thought was Norman Angell's book *The Great Illusion* which, immediately on publication in 1909, ran through several editions in Britain and innumerable translations and editions abroad. It sought to show that the economic and financial interdependence between nations would make war both unprofitable and unfeasible, and that it was therefore illusory to plan for or to fear one. To a large extent, he was correct: the logic of economic progress, the overwhelming interest of the peoples of Europe, lay in peace and further economic integration and mutual dependence. But the illusion was Angell's, believing that governments would act in the true interests of their people, or that chauvinistic sentiments, once called up from the depths, would be diverted by economic or material or even humanitarian considerations. War did break out, and, save for a small minority, the socialist parties and the other protagonists of international understanding joined the majorities of their countries in warlike and 'patriotic' fervour. In August 1914, the economic progress and integration of a century appeared to be in danger of total reversal.

67 *Speculators*, drawing by Otto Dix, 1923, to emphasize the massive inflation of the period.

VI THE THREAT OF
ECONOMIC DISINTEGRATION
1919–1945

The First World War of 1914–18, titanic in its destructiveness in other spheres of European life, also had powerful disruptive consequences on the economy. Though short in duration by comparison with the previous general European war – the twenty-two years of the French wars, 1793–1815 – it was of far greater intensity. No trading with the enemy on this occasion, no transmission of one's gold to the safety of his frontiers, no speculation in his government loans. The severance of economic links, the blockade, was total, just at a time when mutual economic interdependence had become greater than ever before. The engagement of economic resources in the struggle, the material losses incurred, were also immeasurably greater than on any previous occasion.

Yet the resources of the modern state were also greater. Food was rationed, ships were commandeered, labour was conscripted and factories controlled. Apart from Russia, there were no famines or pestilences such as had accompanied earlier wars, during the fighting. They began only after the fighting had stopped, and traditional authority had broken down over a large part of Europe. In many respects, the early years of the peace were worse than the war that had preceded it.

The Allies' peace terms included the right of national self-determination, at least among the subject nations of the losers, and this right, which became a rallying cry in several revolutions in central and eastern Europe, even before any formal peace treaties were concluded, led to substantial changes in the frontiers of Europe by the break-up of the Austro-Hungarian and the Russian Empires. After five new states had been carved out of the western marches of Russia, and the Austro-Hungarian empire had been parcelled out among seven states, several of them new ones, the result was that the number of customs units in Europe had been increased from twenty to twenty-seven, and, when the losses of territory of Germany were taken into account, the frontiers of Europe had been lengthened by 7,000 miles.

What made matters worse was that these new territorial units broke up naturally complementary economic regions, cut off cities from their rural hinterland and cut across established lines of communication, so that the Czechoslovak railways, for example, still centred on Vienna rather than on Prague; in addition their governments began at once to 'protect' their industries, mines or agriculture by keeping out products of former suppliers, and when they had none to protect, proceeded to create them by artificial stimuli. Such policies, once begun, led to understandable similar defensive reactions by other nations. In contrast with the newly created nation state of the nineteenth century which enlarged the economic area and operated in the direction of expansion and progress, the newly created nation state of the twentieth century became a fetter on efficiency and progress, and lent its power to the turning back of the wheels of history.

69 Opposite, *The* ▶ *Match-seller* (1921), painting by Otto Dix, a bitter comment on the post-war economic climate in Germany.

68 Map showing the territorial changes in Europe brought about by the First World War: numerous new international boundaries were created, often cutting across existing lines of communication.

Similarly, while the former, typified by the unification of Germany and Italy, seemed to be fulfilling the destiny of a long and uninterrupted historical evolution, the latter entered upon their heritage in a psychological atmosphere of insecurity, rancour, uncertain frontiers and dissatisfied national minorities, and in consequence their search for autarky tended to be unusually aggressive and uncompromising. In the first post-war years this contributed to the fall in incomes and output, and the widespread famine and epidemic conditions.

The rest of Europe, too, emerged from the war in 1918 with much of its economic fabric shattered. Russia was given over to revolution, counter-revolution, foreign invasion and civil war and needed many years before it again became a major producer and trading partner. The industrialized nations of the west had lost many of their traditional overseas markets for their manufactures, as in the absence of European supplies the latter had begun to learn to manage for themselves. Britain lost or sold a quarter of her overseas investments, France a half, Germany virtually all of them. Germany also lost a large part of her mineral resources, her fleet and most of her mercantile marine, while the Allies were left with a greatly expanded shipbuilding capacity which was soon to lead to a crisis of over-production. Massive panic migrations occurred as a result of the political changes, usually by people with few assets and little hope: over a million

Germans from the lost eastern territories, perhaps 1·5 million Russian *émigrés*, while about 3 million Greeks, Turks and Bulgars were exchanged as the result of the Lausanne Convention. By contrast, the formerly free movement of people following economic opportunities, and of capital, across existing frontiers was sharply curtailed, while new frontiers severed former areas of free exchange. The reductions on immigration into the USA beginning in 1920 were felt particularly severely. Perhaps most significant, the abandonment of the gold standard in the war had allowed different degrees of inflation to take place in different countries, and the resulting uncertainties about the value of money reduced foreign trade and investment, created hyperinflation in some areas and paved the way for competitive exchange manipulations in others.

Even so, something of the pre-war environment of economic expansion and international peace might have been restored fairly quickly. In sheer physical terms the devastation caused by the fighting in northern France and Belgium was made good in a remarkably brief time; a 'restocking' boom replaced much capital equipment in 1919–20; industrial output soon began to rise and would have continued to rise faster if a market had been assured. Similarly, savings recommenced wherever conditions stabilized. American relief prevented the worst of the starvation and primed the pumps in 1918–19, safeguarded capitalism by countering Socialist politicians and, in the 1920s, American capital poured into Europe, particularly Germany, to finance the modernization of industry.

There were many signs of resumed international co-operation after the war, even with formerly enemy countries; indeed the experience of the war itself led many to pursue the paths of peace in order to ensure that it would never happen again. This was particularly so in questions in which there was no direct conflict between states. Thus international financial conferences in Brussels (1920) and Genoa (1922) attempted to restabilize currencies. Successful financial reorganizations were carried out, with the help of British and American capital, in Austria (1922) and Hungary (1924), while in 1925 there were stabilization loans to Poland, Czechoslovakia, Bulgaria, Italy and Roumania. After Germany's hyperinflation, her *Reichsmark* was stabilized in 1923–24 with the help of the international Dawes Plan and associated loans.

Apart from the newly founded League of Nations, International Labour Office and their associated organizations, the pre-war practical international conventions and agreements were resumed or extended, covering ever more areas of economic and social life as society and technology became more complex. Thus an International Chamber of Commerce was formed in 1920 to seek to apply unemotional rational principles of business to international economic policy, and to deal with such practical questions of international economic relations as double taxation, commercial arbitration, customs formalities and 'most-favoured-nation' clauses. The World Economic Conference of 1927 spoke out strongly in favour of the general lowering of tariff duties, and a few tariff rates were in fact lowered before the economic blizzard beginning in 1929 and the American Hawley-Smoot Act drove them up again. A proposed customs union between Germany and Austria in 1931 was vetoed by the French for political reasons, and the plans for a customs union between Holland, Belgium and Luxembourg made at Ouchy in 1932 ran into British opposition for allegedly violating the most-favoured-nation provisions, but in 1934 the five Scandinavian governments (including Iceland) set up 'Delegations for the Promotion of Economic Co-operation between the Northern Countries' which had some modest success. The enlargement of the German customs area by the swallowing up of Austria and Czechoslovakia in 1938–39 can hardly be included in the same category.

International cartels resumed their activities after the war with renewed vigour and over a much wider field. There was an even more marked expansion of the international company with branches and manufacturing plants in many countries, particularly in the new industries like chemicals, electrical engineering and cars (Courtaulds, Unilever, ICI, GEC (USA), EMI, Ford, General Motors), in retailing (Woolworth, Debenhams, C & A) and, as ever, in oil, banking and insurance. Among labour organizations existing international links were maintained and given strength by the growth of national trade unions and socialist parties, but the split between the communists and the rest fatally reduced the weight which they carried in political terms.

Those who were hoping for peace and international understanding, and for picking up the threads of economic progress after the Armistice of 1918, might perhaps have been forgiven for thinking that the pre-war developments would continue in a benign way, the fighting and the peace treaties having purged Europe once and for all of the causes of conflict, since the superficial signs pointed in that direction. But those who could discern the underlying reality were bound to come to very different conclusions. From the economic point of view, the peace settlements had left the political framework in a far more adverse position than before towards the needs of the people of Europe and the inner urge towards expansion and progress which the system of western capitalism had generated in the past. In a dozen different ways the peace treaties and their political consequences thwarted, hampered and obstructed the economy of Europe in a manner which had not been seen since the Industrial and the French revolutions. At the same time, in the complex symbiosis in which the economic and the political affect each other, the capitalist economy itself appeared to have lost its capacity for expansion and adaptation, and to lurch into an unprecedented and apparently insoluble crisis, whether because of its own inner laws or because of the political responses it had stimulated. Certainly, that crisis increased the strain on the political framework, and provoked reactions in it which affected the economy of Europe even more adversely in turn. The war, far from having cured the sickness of modern industrialized Europe, was found to have aggravated its causes.

The story is a complex one to unravel and here we can pursue only some of its strands. One of the threads was the reparations clause of the Treaty of Versailles. In past wars the payment of an 'indemnity' by the vanquished to the victor had occasionally been one of the spoils of war, and the French milliards paid to Germany after the war of 1870 were still fresh in the minds of European diplomats as an example of a payment which greatly benefited the receiver. But the First World War had brought with it a different order of destructiveness. Calculations by the victors, propelled forward by an inflamed public opinion, of damage done to the Allies by the war and the German occupation of their territory produced astronomical sums that bore no relation to Germany's capacity to pay, still less to transfer in foreign currency. The effects of these inflated demands after some initial payments in kind in repairs to the devastated areas and post-war occupation costs, were not only worthless, they were seriously counter-productive.

To begin with, as no agreement could be reached on the precise figure to be demanded, Germany was asked to pay without a finite end in sight. A global sum of 132 milliard gold marks (£6,500 million), fixed in 1921, was little better because of its unrealistic enormity. It not only caused resentment in Germany and the beginning of that hatred of the *Diktat* of the Versailles Treaty which was before long

70 A German
view of the
economic crisis of
1931.

again to shatter the peace of Europe; it also placed unusual burdens on the German government and contributed to its loss of control in an inflation of astronomical proportions (in 1923 a million million depreciated marks equalled one old one), though it has also been argued that the government was not sorry to see that inflation as a form of repudiating its debts. A hold-up in reparations payments also led the French and Belgians to occupy the Ruhr in 1923, with consequent loss of production, local passive resistance and a heritage of bitterness, but without an increased flow of resources to France. The attempts of successive German democratic governments to meet at least part of their obligations aggravated the slump of 1930–32, with its massive deflation and unemployment, and these in turn were a major cause of the growth of extremist nationalist parties which blamed the foreigner for German troubles and gained popularity by promising to repudiate these obligations. The fact was that Germany, having lost a large part of her minerals, most of her overseas holdings and her large ships, and having suffered more industrial dislocations and destruction than most of the other belligerents, was in no position to make large surpluses available and could not meet her import bill by exports, even without finding resources for reparations. In any case, even if Germany could have raised the resources, the 'transfer problem' would have prevented their payment, for the Allies, afraid of unemployment for their own industries, were not in a position to accept the only kinds of commodities in which such payments could have been made. The matter was aggravated by the American insistence on repayment of the war-time loans to her Allies, so that the French, in particular, were dependent on reparations from Germany in order to make their payments to the USA.

The inflation of 1923 marked the total breakdown of these arrangements, and the Dawes Plan of September 1924 appeared to offer a way out. It settled German payments on a more realistic, lower scale of £50 million a year at first rising to £125 million later, and it settled its share-out among the recipients, though there was still no terminal date. In the next few years, as the Locarno Pact of 1925 promised peace, and the re-established gold standard in Britain (1925) and elsewhere promised financial stability, Germany actually balanced her budget and made payments under the Dawes Plan, which allowed other countries to meet their obligations in turn. But appearances were misleading. The German payments, the apparent fountainhead of this stream of settlements, were not raised in Germany, but were in turn the result of foreign loans, particularly from America. In 1924–31 Germany drew some £1,000 million from abroad and the irony was that Germany, in fact, received far more in loans including loans to enable her to pay interest on earlier loans than she paid out in reparations, thus gaining in the circular flow and re-equipping her industries and her public utilities with American funds in the process in the 1920s before repudiating her debts in the 1930s. Meanwhile, however, this system of large payments across the frontiers without any real transactions to represent them had two major adverse consequences. One was the obstruction to normal trade and the difficulty of lowering tariffs in these fluctuating conditions. The other was the danger inherent in the dependence of the system on continued investment by the USA, and in the German practice of borrowing on short term but investing in long-term capital. As soon as American lending began to tail off in 1928, first because investors were induced to feed the stock exchange boom at home in 1928–29, and then as a result of the crisis and depression when American capital even began to be repatriated, the sudden imbalance in the payments circle served to aggravate the European economic crisis by a major financial collapse.

Another post-war weakness arose from the change from a world gold standard based on one strong centre, London, to a system with two foci, London and New York. The existence of two centres, with potentially conflicting policies, was itself a disadvantage. It was much aggravated by the fact that New York, while it took over some of London's pre-1914 role as world banker and lender, omitted one vital feature of the pre-war British economy: free trade at home. American protection remained high, repayments to the USA by way of imports there remained obstructed, and the dollar was therefore inclined to become an unnaturally hard currency and to be overvalued, with further adverse effects on international trade. When the dollar was finally devalued in 1933 it was too late to help American employment, but destructive to European recovery. Meanwhile London, the other focus, remained too weak to bear the burden of the pound sterling as a major reserve currency. This weakness was accentuated by a proud insistence on returning to gold at the old parity in 1925–31, which seriously weakened the competitive powers of British export industries, and by the lavish support to various other European currencies after the war, partly in opposition to the French, a luxury for which British resources proved inadequate. The financial collapse of Austria and Germany in 1931 then quickly dragged down London, too, which had lent heavily on short term to Germany; and with sterling off the gold standard a new high protectionist policy in Britain became inevitable and provided a strong incentive to further obstructions to trade all round. The French franc stabilization of 1928 at an undervalued parity led to a large inflow of gold to Paris, where it was hoarded and used to isolate the French economy from the world's unemployment, instead of being available in the vulnerable financial centres to stave off general financial collapse. Most of the remainder of the world's gold migrated to the USA where it was not allowed to influence circulation, so that its loss caused contraction of employment elsewhere while its gain did not cause expansion of employment or imports in the USA.

The high level of unemployment itself was another adverse factor which tended in general to induce illiberal policies. After the post-war speculative boom ending in 1920 most European countries experienced a drastic slump and, although it was followed by a rapid recovery of output to 1925 and a boom of classic intensity to 1929, a hard core of unemployment remained, particularly in Germany and in Britain. In part this was the result of war-time dislocations of markets and industries, of over-expansion in some sectors and the decline of traditional methods in others, and may therefore be attributed to slow structural adaptation. But it began to look as though, unlike the pre-war years, Europe would have to get used to a large pool of unemployed workers at every phase of the trade cycle. No government could face the emerging social and political pressures with equanimity, and protective policies which promised to benefit employment at home were therefore growing in favour.

AGRICULTURE

Perhaps the most difficult and intractable problem of structural adaptation was that faced by agriculture and the production of primary products. The war had seen a drastic reduction in food output, particularly in central and eastern Europe, as male labour had gone off to the war, horses were requisitioned, artificial fertilizers were hard to come by and, in the latter years, the seed grain and the breeding stocks began to be consumed. The overseas countries rose magnificently to the occasion and made up a great part of the shortfall, but in the 1920s European agriculture, using new machinery and better techniques, revived remarkably quickly, and its yield began to exceed pre-war figures in terms of output per acre and output per worker. Thus from the mid-1920s on a food surplus began to threaten world markets.

The following statistics relating to the production and imports of wheat (1 quintal = 100 kilograms) will illustrate the change:

Average annual production (million quintals)

Years	World (excluding Europe and Russia)	Europe (excluding Russia)	European net imports
1909–13	453	370	114
1925–29	629	368	143
1930–34	567	413	136
1935–36	548	415	80

A number of historical and institutional factors made it much more difficult to deal with the threatened glut than would have been the case in earlier decades. First, the population growth in Europe, the main import-consuming area, had slowed down dramatically, in part because of the loss of lives and of potential births during the war. Moreover, what growth there was occurred in south-eastern Europe, which was itself a food-exporting area. Added to this was the long-term effect of Engel's Law according to which ever smaller shares of rising incomes were devoted to food among the consumers of western Europe in this period.

The particular structure of agriculture and its political and social role also worked against an easy resolution of the problem of the surplus. The experience of the blockade and the hunger years was not likely to make governments underrate the importance of autarky in food, of being independent of foreign supplies. Thus, as food prices began to fall, the importing countries raised their protective barriers to preserve the strength of the agrarian sector even though this raised home costs. When that proved inadequate, they poured subsidies both into the farms and into the processing industries like sugar-refining and spirit-distilling. Germany reacted first in 1925 and Italy had her 'battle of wheat', but most other countries followed in the slump of 1929–31 and even Britain from 1932 onwards. The central and eastern European food producers who had gone a long way towards wrecking their regional economy by insisting on building up their own industries at great sacrifice, competing with each other and with their pre-war suppliers, were yet, by the peasant structure of their agriculture, not thereby reducing their food surpluses. Thus the European food producers kept on increasing their output while their western markets shrank and the overseas producers, too, being mostly farmers, tended to react to lower prices by trying to sell more rather than produce less, thus pushing prices down still further. Whereas industry had increasing unemployment, agriculture had increasing poverty.

It remains to be added that this 'over-production' affected a large number of primary products, such as tin, copper and rubber, as well as food like wheat, sugar and coffee. It was, of course, only relative over-production: millions of people went hungry while coffee was burnt up in locomotives and grain harvests held back, but it proved to be the kind of maladjustment that seemed to benefit neither buyer nor seller, but instead drove both into restrictive measures which lowered output, incomes and international trade in an ever-tightening vicious spiral.

After the boom of 1920 world prices took a downward turn, but prices of food and raw materials fell faster than prices of manufactures. The 'terms of trade' thus turned against primary producers, and by protecting their own, the European importers tried to shift the burden of the crisis on to the overseas and eastern European suppliers. Countries who lived by converting imported cattle-feeds into meat, like Denmark, Ireland or Switzerland, had the gain from falling grain prices to offset against falling sale prices of meat, but grain producers (like overseas producers of cotton, tea or coffee) suffered without compensation. On the face of it the changing terms of trade looked like a good bargain for the industrial countries, and they did, indeed, benefit by higher real consumption. But if their traditional suppliers were prevented from exporting their food, they could not then buy the manufactured goods in return and where, as in the case of many British colonies and dominions, they had large annual interest payments to make in constant money while prices fell, they might be driven to stop payment altogether. European agricultural countries, like Denmark, Holland or Switzerland were encouraged to start up their own industries, reducing the European division of labour still further and spreading more unemployment among Europe's industry.

The price fall was sharpest during the worst depression years of 1929–32, and was unprecedented in modern times, in spite of the most elaborate schemes and accumulations of stocks held off the market. For the world's agricultural commodities, the index of stocks and prices compared as follows (1923–25 = 100):

Year	Stocks	Prices
1927	146	81
end 1929	193	64
1932	262	24

With stocks two and a half times higher, prices had fallen to one-quarter, wrecking in seven years not only innumerable farm economies, but also a great deal of the world's exchange system built up over the previous century.

MONETARY POLICY AND INTERNATIONAL TRADE

The depression which set in in 1929 was the worst suffered by modern capitalistic Europe to that date, whether measured by the decline in output or the level of unemployment. It is clear that the long-term disorganization of the European economy sketched here in its main features contributed to the gravity of the crisis while being itself aggravated by it. What is most significant for our purposes is that every major economic consideration tended to push countries in the same direction: to seek salvation by reducing imports, or attempting to expand exports. The adverse trade balances suffered by many countries (including Britain) naturally had this effect – while countries with trade surpluses were afraid to allow these to increase their

71 *In Front of the Labour Exchange*, painting by Grete Jürgens, 1929.

home prices, and provided no countervailing expansion. It was equally reasonable to seek to deal with unemployment by the same means, for every pound exported helped to create a job at home, while every pound imported helped to extinguish one. Countries with fixed obligations, either arising out of foreign investments, or reparations, as in the case of Germany, had to try to achieve a 'surplus' to transfer them, while countries due to receive them tried to keep out the commodities with which these payments could alone be made. Gold reserves could be protected only by the same means, by boosting exports and discouraging imports. The causes might be dissimilar, but the effect was in each case to encourage a twentieth-century form of mercantilism.

It is clear that these neo-mercantilist policies were mutually self-defeating. Moreover, in view of the power of foreign governments to counteract any attempt to expand exports, the tendency was to use the easier and safer means of keeping out imports instead: thus each account was 'balanced' in turn by reduction, not expansion, to be followed by other consequential reductions. To be sure, there were attempts to stave off this beggar-my-neighbour policy by national agreements but they could not hold up the decline: these included the Young Plan for German reparations in 1929 which lowered annual payments still further and for the first time set a finite period

143

for payments, to end in 1988; or Hoover's moratorium (June 1931) on loan repayments for one year, which allowed payments all round to be suspended, as it turned out, for good; the Stresa Conference of 1932, which attempted to liberalize trade; and the London Monetary and Economic Conference of 1933, which ended in failure. There was no lack of goodwill or of initiative to stem the adverse tide. A conference, mostly of European powers, met in 1930 and while it could not agree on a tariff truce – to abstain from raising tariffs for one year – eighteen signatories undertook to prolong existing commercial agreements until 1931 and not to raise statutory tariffs until then. The Lausanne Conference of 1932 attempted to deal with the transfer problem of the central and eastern European countries and called for a world conference to revive international trade, which became the conference of 1935; and the Committee of Economic Experts set up by the European Commission in 1931 also made plans for benefiting production and trade in Europe. There were also several abortive regional European conferences with the same objective, but the framework within which they operated did not allow them to succeed, and this included mounting unemployment, distress and social unrest at home, and the need to protect one's country abroad, maintaining the basic diplomatic assumption of putting its interest above that of the world community as a whole.

Thus as employment and income fell, trade fell much more in the worst years. But even when production began to recover, the apparatus of restriction was not lifted: it now appeared as a permanent handicap to be carried in good times and bad. The effect was particularly striking in the case of foodstuffs and manufactured goods, as shown in the following comparative world index figures for the boom year 1929 (= 100 in each case) with the worst year of the depression (1932) and the peak of the next boom (1937):

		Quantities (1929 = 100) in	
		1932	*1937*
Foodstuffs:	trade	89	93·5
	production	100	108
Raw materials:	trade	81·5	108
	production	74	116
Manufactures:	trade	59·5	87
	production	70	120

144   In monetary terms, the decline in trade was of course much greater.

The dissection of Europe into its component parts, each trying so far as possible to live an independent existence, was achieved not merely by tariffs, as before 1914. The modern state disposed an armoury of new weapons, many of which were not only more effective, but also more destructive. The raising of tariffs was, however, still generally the first step.

Among the larger countries, we have seen the American Hawley-Smoot Act of 1930 drastically raising rates and thereby ending all hopes among European countries of meeting their dollar obligations. Germany, after its agrarian tariff of 1925, raised rates further, until rye carried a duty of 300 per cent. In France, as world wheat prices fell, the wheat duty was raised to 200 per cent. For agricultural imports as a whole, the average rates of all French imports rose from $4\frac{1}{2}$ per cent in the 1920s to $10\frac{1}{2}$ per cent by 1933, and for manufactured imports, from 11 to 17 per cent. The close customs union of 1928 between Metropolitan France and the rest of her empire further reduced foreign imports. The most drastic change occurred in Great Britain: the free-trade tradition of nearly a century had survived with only minor modifications, but it was jettisoned unceremoniously by a tariff in 1932 which began by a rate of 20 per cent on most manufactured imports (up to 33 per cent on some) and 10 per cent on most semi-manufactures and foodstuffs. The preferential rates for Commonwealth countries negotiated at Ottawa later in the year generally entailed the raising of rates to foreign importers.

Smaller countries followed suit. There was quick retaliation against American goods in Italy and Spain in 1930 and an unofficial boycott of American goods in Italy and Switzerland. Italian grain tariffs rose faster than those of France, though not as high as the German. Countries like Denmark, Holland and Switzerland graded their tariff rates carefully to favour their own advanced agriculture without raising its costs. Others introduced finely calibrated 'multiple-column' tariffs, to favour imports from countries which offered favours in return without thereby opening the gates wide to others. The Greek tariffs on goods from non-treaty countries were ten times as high as those on imports from countries with which commercial treaties had been concluded.

However, in view of the drastic price falls, particularly of primary products, tariffs were frequently felt to be inadequate. They could also be neutralized and were so in many cases, as for example in the case of sugar, by open or disguised export subsidies. In the case of

145

Poland, nearly half the revenue of her agrarian exporters arose out of export subsidies by the Polish state. Therefore many countries turned to the cruder but more direct methods of the quota, or quantitative restrictions. France applied them to about half the number of items in her tariff list between 1931 and 1934, setting them in many cases at half the previous quantities imported. Significantly, many of these restrictions were lifted when France went off the gold standard in 1936. Other countries operating these restrictions were Germany, Switzerland and the Netherlands. In Germany quotas were given for imports at a favoured rate, the rest of imports having to bear the full tariff, and the same applied to import quotas under the European steel cartel. By the end of 1932 there were fifteen countries and by 1939 nineteen countries in Europe (and twenty-eight the world over) which were operating quotas or licensing systems. Quota restrictions could be aggregate, or divided up among the importing countries, and these shares, expressed in absolute quantities, could then be used as a basis for bilateral trade and barter agreements.

A related procedure for a government seeking to improve its trade balance was to apply pressure to countries with which it had a favourable balance, for which, in other words, it formed an important market, to take more in return. Thus Britain, as the main purchaser of Danish bacon, could insist on getting a much larger share of Danish coal imports in return. If successful, this kind of move would lead to displacement elsewhere, say a reduction in Danish coal imports from Germany, and the country hit in this way might retaliate in similar manner – Germany, for example, driving British coal out of Mediterranean countries by similar means. The end result was a break-up of one of the finest achievements of the nineteenth-century Europe and world economy, a network of multilateral trade, into sets of bilateral trade agreements, and this further disorganized Europe, forced purchasers into patronizing inferior sources of supply, and reduced overall trade – all for the sake of mutually incompatible attempts to 'balance' foreign payments. Large parts of Europe virtually reverted to a barter economy, negating in this sense a millennium of progress.

Thus in 1932 and 1933 Germany negotiated for the exchange of 9 million marks' worth of German coal for Brazilian cotton, and German fertilizer for Egyptian cotton. The Polish Company for Compensation Trade began operating in November 1932, but the system spread more rapidly everywhere after the failure of the World

Wählt nationalsozialistisch!
(Hitler-Bewegung)
Streiter-Verlag, Zwickau.

72 A Nazi election poster, 1930, attempting to focus hatred on international high finance as the 'enemy of the world'.

Economic Conference in 1933. Between 1934 and 1938 the USA made twenty foreign bilateral trade agreements. Such bilateral agreements could sometimes increase trade, or at least stave off its decline (though usually at the expense of other countries) and it was for that reason favoured by the newly established Bank for International Settlement in 1931.

In the hands of the German National Socialist government bilateral trade agreements were incorporated into much more complex and even more restrictive 'blocs'. In the case of countries from which Germany needed vital raw materials, or whose markets she required, she adopted a system of paying in blocked accounts, which could be used only on purchases in Germany, or if they were to be converted

147

73 A Dutch cartoon on
protectionist tariffs, 1931.

into free foreign currency for the foreign importer to take out, they
were available only at a heavy discount, at a fraction of the value.
Gradually a whole battery of special marks, at varying rates of discount, developed in 1934–39, and Germany was able to finance a
critical part of her rearmament by these methods of requisition and
repudiation. On the other hand, in the case of countries for which
Germany was a main market and therefore in a strong bargaining
position, i.e. the agricultural producers of eastern and south-eastern
Europe, she obliged her trading partners to take a large share of
Germany's unwanted surplus manufactured output by special clearing
agreements, and these tied them effectively to the German market.
Thus, by the later 1930s, the German economy and its satellites had
become virtually isolated from the rest of Europe, and communicated
with it only through controlled, planned and restricted channels,
managed for the sole purpose of preparing Germany for the war she
considered inevitable. By that time Germany alone among the
western countries suffered from over-full employment and a shortage
of goods, rather than unemployment and a shortage of markets, but
her need to restrict trade in the interest of 'balance' was just as strong.

Other countries developed ingenious systems of production subsidies, particularly in agriculture, in order to transmit some benefits of
cheap world (import) prices to consumers without ruining home
farmers. Britain devised marketing boards, with compulsory levies
and differential pricing, while her Wheat Commission operated a
scheme which used the returns from import duties to subsidize home
farmers. In Holland, farmers were guaranteed high prices for cereals,
achieved by selling to millers a compulsory quota at a higher price
148 than was paid to farmers, the rest being dumped for rough usage at

whatever the market would bear. By this means the Dutch wheat acreage was actually increased from 112,000 acres in 1929 to 380,000 in 1935, at a time of world glut conditions. In the case of potatoes, there were export subsidies, and a proportion was 'denatured', i.e. made unfit for human consumption, in order to relieve the pressure of supplies. France used similar methods for her wheat surplus: in 1933–35, 1·3 million tons were exported and 1·1 million tons denatured. Yet the glut continued, and in 1936 'wheat offices' were set up to buy up all farm sales compulsorily, export and denature what the home market could not absorb, and levy farmers as a whole to bear the cost. French wine-growers were paid by the state for destroying vineyards, as long as no other cash crop was grown on the land; they were fined if their yield per acre was too high, and irrigation was prohibited. In Switzerland, a monopoly commission, first privately run and in 1929 working under the federal government, bought up all the available wheat, sold home-grown wheat compulsorily at a loss to millers and imported wheat at a profit, and covered the deficit by a federal subsidy. Here, too, farmers were encouraged by this system to double the wheat acreage by 1938 (compared with 1914), increasing the share of Swiss home supplies from 20 to 33 per cent. Equally or perhaps even more complex schemes were operated by many other countries, including Sweden, Czechoslovakia and the Baltic republics.

Restrictions on capital and labour movements across frontiers were intensified in this period also, further reducing contacts, and creating additional sources of distrust, instability and rigidity. Many of the larger firms were forced to build branch factories to beat the tariff, but this helped to break up the European economy further rather than cement it together.

Compared with previous ages, however, the most remarkable new development of measures of control and restriction occurred in the financial and monetary sphere. The retreat from the common gold standard – by Britain in 1931, the USA in 1933 and France in 1936, other countries following suit in due course – left the way open for all kinds of ingenious methods of manipulation and discrimination.

We have already noted the bilateral trade treaties which were normally associated with 'clearing agreements' to ensure that payments between any two countries cancelled out in a given period. The next step was to assign different values to one's own currency in these clearing agreements, according to the relative economic weakness of

149

the trading partner, currency becoming a mere arbitrary unit of account instead of a genuine means of payment. The German mark was the chief currency used in this way, losing its status as an international currency in any accepted sense in this period. By autumn 1937 as many as 151 clearing agreements operated between 38 countries, and there were 23 payments agreements between 24 countries in existence.

Other countries became adept at manipulating the exchange value of their currencies in order to keep out imports and boost exports. The French and Belgians had even in the 1920s returned to gold on a much devalued basis, and as a result the French authorities achieved large surpluses and a massive influx of gold. Britain led the field in competitive devaluation in the 1930s, but was closely followed by the USA and it was not until 1936, when France had also devalued, that these three main powers which still maintained some freedom for their currency concluded a Tripartite Agreement to eschew unilateral action of this kind in the future. Yet the monetary uncertainty continued to bedevil and inhibit international trade. Some representative examples of currency fluctuations (December 1929 = 100) are:

	Index of valuation of national currency against the US dollar in			Depreciation against gold
	1932	*1934*	*1938*	*1938*
France	99	168	67	40
Belgium	99	167	120	71
Sweden	66	95	89	53
Switzerland	99	167	116	68
United Kingdom	67	101	96	57

Governments also learnt to limit and rectify their payments deficits by home deflation and unemployment. This once more was self-defeating if indulged by others, each round merely worsening the extent of total unemployment and loss of income which Europe had to carry, without benefit to anyone, but once it was started, the crisis conditions in each country in turn left no other option but to continue competitively downwards in the vain attempt to create some stability for home employment.

Associated with the manipulation of exchange rates were measures of exchange control, the limitation of freedom to obtain foreign exchange and thus to finance imports, and the associated control over foreign investment. We have noted this kind of control in its most drastic form in Germany and it was almost as tight in Poland, whereas in Britain it appeared only in the mild form of an unofficial discouragement to exporting capital outside what was clearly developing into a Sterling Area. Control to prevent the flight of capital could sometimes be counter-productive, leading to panic, and conversely, the restitution of freedom could restore confidence and end the panic, as in Australia, Estonia and Portugal in 1933–34. Although it could be circumvented to some extent by false invoicing, by gold movements and by the purchase and sale of securities, exchange control was a fairly effective means of isolating individual economies from the world economy, sometimes for the purpose of raising prices and employment at home, and breaking up European linkages still further. By controlling all available foreign exchange, and rationing it in accordance with some general policy, the central monetary authorities could also make exchange control into a further means of strengthening bilateral relationships at the expense of multilateral world commerce. In 1931 twenty-one countries had introduced exchange control and in 1932–38 twenty-five more were added to the list. By the mid-1930s, at least five separate currency areas had evolved (not counting Soviet Russia or the underdeveloped world) in place of the single payments area before 1914: the Sterling Area, including northern Europe and the Commonwealth; the Dollar Area of North and South America; the Gold Bloc of western Europe, then in dissolution, led by France; the Exchange Control Area of central Europe, tied to Germany; and Japan and the Far East. Although the first three attempted to create bridges between them after 1936, the absence of a single focus (or even of two) made any world multilateralism all the more difficult. In the 1930s net capital outflow from the lender countries had ceased: such capital movements as there were were mainly repayments by the international borrowers.

All the various measures described here have to be seen as a single battery of weapons, reinforcing, supporting, protecting or, for that matter, neutralizing each other. The overall intention, achieved with remarkable success, was the isolation of each country from the rest, the reduction of each country's dependence on foreign trade and payments. The achievements of those goals were all the more remarkable if it is remembered that they ran directly against the trend of the previous century of slow evolution.

Thus for Europe as a whole (excluding Russia), while the volume of commodity production rose by 15 per cent from 1913 to 1928, and by a further 15 per cent in 1928–38, the volume of intra-European trade remained constant in the first phase, and declined in the second by 10 per cent. Among the leading industrial countries, while production of manufactures rose by 65 per cent in 1913–29 and by 9 per cent in 1929–37, imports rose in the first phase by only 22 per cent, and in the second they fell by 29 per cent. For individual countries, in consequence, foreign trade fell drastically as a share of national income and exports fell as a proportion of manufacturing output:

	Foreign trade as percentage of national income in			Manufactures exported (per cent) in		
	1913	1928	1938	1913	1929	1937
United Kingdom	59·3	49·1	28·3	45	37	21
Germany	41·6	36·0	14·6	31	27	15
France	42·5	46·4	21·3	26	25	12
Italy	29·5	30·5	16·6	18	23	21
Belgium	—	113·5	68·4			
Netherlands	—	77·6	51·7			
Sweden	56·8	41·7	35·3			

The trade that suffered particularly was triangular trade, as each country tried to balance each of its relationships separately, and trade among the more advanced industrial countries, which lost in relation to the non-European world. The countries with the greatest contraction of trade were those with the highest unemployment rates, Germany and Britain, as well as France which used the quota system most drastically, but above all the USA. While, in current dollars, actual world imports (outside the USA) dropped to 40 per cent of the 1929 level by 1932, US imports dropped to 30 per cent; and while they recovered elsewhere in the boom of 1937 to 78 per cent of their top 1929 level, in the US they rose only to 50 per cent.

It was as if the German economists who claimed to have discovered a 'law', according to which the share of trade in national income would fall as a country developed, turned out to be right after all. The doctrine had emerged at the same time about the turn of the century as the debate on *Agrarstaat* versus *Industriestaat* – whether Germany should allow her agriculture to decline, like Britain, so as to become a purely industrial state, or whether she should make the effort to preserve a more balanced economy. The bigots who thought in terms of German military power rather than in terms of the prosperity of the people of Europe had apparently won out.

The cost of this regression, the damage done to Europe, went far beyond the material or economic. Europe had not only to bear the cost of idle men and machines, of purchases forced into uneconomic channels, of an end to the freedom of movement which had been one of the finest achievements of the nineteenth century. Another cost was the social demoralization, the breakdown of civic virtues, of democratic attitudes and forms of government, that occurred within the individual states of Europe. But what turned out to be most destructive of all in the end was the building up of political tensions, the battle for survival by each state separately, and the growing contempt for international agreement, for all these caught the countries of Europe in a net which dragged them inexorably into a Second World War in 1939, continuing a struggle that had begun in 1914 but not finished in 1918.

In the expansive days of the mid-nineteenth century the adherents of the 'Manchester School' had believed that the growing economic integration arising from free trade would guarantee peace by first reducing tendencies to chauvinism and then making each country too dependent on the supplies of the others to allow it to go to war with them. That view, propounded once more with even greater optimism by Norman Angell just before the First World War broke out, proved to be too simple and too optimistic. It neglected, among others, the tensions, envy and hostility arising from the uneven stages of development, and consequent unequal success in imperialist expansion, reached by different nations at one time; it neglected the power of nationalism, the inner tensions of a capitalist economy, the tendency of politicians to despise rational economic calculations. Yet there was something in their view, and the converse of their propositions seemed to have a firmer foundation in historical reality: the quest for autarchy and self-sufficiency, the rampant nationalism in many parts of Europe, the neglect of economic sense in the pursuit of the irrational, while by no means furnishing the whole explanation, have their share in the disaster which once again broke over Europe in the form of the Second World War of 1939–45.

74 A French poster issued in 1950, urging the material benefits to be derived from American aid under the Marshall Plan.

VII RECONSTRUCTION SINCE 1945

The Second World War had been more truly a world war than that of 1914–18. Europe, to be sure, was still one of the major battlefields and the collapse of Germany's resistance heralded the end of the conflict, since after it the defeat of the remaining Axis partner, Japan, became merely a matter of time. But the balance of world forces left in the wake of the fighting was very different from the previous occasion. No longer did the states of Europe see the peaceful relationship among themselves as the main component of world peace, or their politics as the determinants of world politics. On the contrary, it became clear very quickly that they had been enfeebled to such an extent that their main concern now was to attract any consideration at all among the great powers. Even such international bodies as the United Nations, which did not yet fully take into account the shift in the relation of forces, gave much greater weight than any earlier organization to such non-European powers as the USA and China, while within Europe the centre of gravity moved to the two states traditionally least or most doubtfully associated with the European idea, the Soviet Union and the United Kingdom. This tendency of the loss of influence of Europe became more evident still in the following years.

The loss of great-power status on the European continent weakened the urge to continue the traditional political game and, by allowing interest in economic welfare to re-emerge into prominence, it helped indirectly in the new drive towards integration. Another factor was the revival of the older political dream of the unity of Europe, which had never entirely disappeared from the European consciousness, even in the unfavourable conditions between the two world wars. For a brief time the pan-European idea propagated by Count Richard Coudenhove-Kalergi had found much support, and in 1929 and 1930 it reached as far as Briand, at times Prime Minister and Foreign Minister of France, who put proposals for a federal Europe before the League of Nations. But his own death soon after that of Stresemann, the depression and the rise of Nazism in Germany, ended the hope of any such development almost as soon as it was formulated. In any case, there was no serious organization, no mass party, no centre of real power behind the idea, and such new forces of European co-operation as the rising international cartels of the time could scarcely be claimed by the federalist idealists as desirable harbingers of the integration of Europe.

In the war which followed German arms conquered most of the Continent and dominated or overawed the remainder, but it would be hard to find behind this forcible integration any conscious plan other than the wish that Germans should control enough land to secure their own food supply, and should weaken and dominate as many subject peoples as possible, particularly among those speaking non-Germanic languages. Hitler's 'New Order' for Europe was a sham in spite of some attempts by supporters like Paul Herre to find a meaning behind it. In the short term there was not even any decision how to exploit the potential of Occupied Europe for the war, whether by the methods of Sauckel, which involved the importation of labour into Germany, or by those of Speer, which attempted to use the productive capabilities of the subject nations on the spot. Neither method was applied consistently or efficiently. For the long term, there was no plan at all, not even a decision on boundaries. The Allies, for their part, prodded by the jealousies of the European governments in exile, and moved by the fear of potential commercial rivalry and by the wish to counter Hitler's New Order by opposing principles, went out of their way to stress their support for the independence of the established nation states of Europe.

Significantly, however, those on the spot thought otherwise. The common experience of defeat and enemy occupation had made the common fate of Europe loom large in their eyes, while it had diminished the value of their separateness. The Resistance leaders, meeting in secret in Switzerland in 1944, strongly supported a post-war European federation. When the fighting ended in 1945, and men surveyed their devastated countries, conscious of the mass movement of refugees across the frontiers, and the common need for aid from the west to survive the next few years, similar value judgments tended to prevail. There was an upsurge of 'European' sentiment, and groupings of the most varied political backgrounds, Catholic, Liberal, Socialist, and of none, formed organizations for greater European integration. Some of the most influential political figures of the day supported this movement, including Léon Blum, Salvador de Madariaga and Winston Churchill. The latter's address to the University of Zurich in 1946 calling for a United States of Europe found a widespread echo in many countries. A poll of 4,200 parliamentarians, of whom 40 per cent replied, showed that only 3 per cent were opposed to federation on principle; in Italy, France, Belgium and the Netherlands over half the lower house deputies favoured some form of federal union. Even General de Gaulle envisaged an 'association between Slavs, Germans, Gauls and Latins'.

However, behind this apparent unanimity a very significant division of views began to appear almost at once. The British and the Scandinavians, who had suffered least from occupation and destruction, were in the end unwilling to submit to any real loss of sovereignty: even Churchill refused in 1951 to lead his country into a European federation. Out of this type of sentiment grew the Consultative Council of Europe, a significant institution which became a sounding-board for ideas and a means of achieving compromises between nations, but a body without powers which left the sovereignty of its member nations intact. It met in Strasbourg for the first time in 1949 under the presidency of Paul-Henri Spaak, the Belgian Socialist leader, and has continued to the present, its membership confined to the non-Communist part of Europe.

By contrast, many leaders of France, Germany and Italy and the smaller states surrounding them were contemplating a more genuine pooling of sovereignty, in which urgent economic needs and industrial requirements were to play a much larger role. It was not without significance that so many of the leading figures should in their own lives have felt the ill-effects of the rigidity of frontiers coupled with the fickleness of their actual location: de Gasperi, the Italian, had sat in an Austrian Parliament; Robert Schuman, the Frenchman, had been reared in German in Alsace; Konrad Adenauer, the German Rhinelander, had seen his province occupied by French troops.

There was yet a third, more immediate factor, to bring Europe closer together in the post-war years: this was the establishment of Communist governments in the east, while economic breakdown threatened in the west. These came to a head in 1947–48, as Prague became openly Communist, as Berlin was blockaded by the Russians in retaliation against the West German currency reform, as the Cominform was set up among the eastern countries but included the Communist Parties of France and Italy, and as Britain declared herself unable any longer to intervene against the Communists in the Greek civil war or to support Turkey. To deal with the strategic part of these events, the United States announced the 'Truman doctrine' of resistance to Communism and proceeded to build up a military alliance against the Soviets in Europe. This became the North Atlantic Treaty Organization (NATO) in 1949.

Economically, the false boom of the early months of peace was followed by severe economic hardships as food and raw materials ran short, reconstruction was held up for lack of them, and one after another the former belligerents found that they could not afford the necessary dollar imports from North America which might have helped them to prime the pumps and get their economies going again. It was clear to most observers that in the long run the European economy was sound, but its more immediate problems could not be overcome because of a general dollar shortage. In this situation the United States offered help that was both swift and adequate. Their plan was announced by General George Marshall, the US Secretary of State, in June 1947. Accordingly, a Convention for European Economic Co-operation met in April 1948 to set up the Organization for European Economic Co-operation (OEEC) of sixteen, later eighteen countries, mainly for the purpose of distributing the American funds, but also to find ways of facilitating trade and payment among themselves. Despite its title, the OEEC was from its beginning not wholly orientated towards Europe, and in 1960 it became the Organization for Economic Co-operation and Development (OECD) which specifically included Canada and the USA as well as the European partners.

Within its set limits the Marshall Plan was successful. Some $12,500 million was spent under the Economic Co-operation Act in less than four years, and by the end of 1953 American aid to Europe had reached $23,400 million ($7,700 million for military, $15,700 million for economic assistance). Communism was contained in the East and pushed back in the West, and the advanced countries in Europe were set on a path of unprecedented and, at the time, unimaginable economic growth and prosperity. As their dollar shortage was eased, restrictions on mutual trade and payments between them could be lifted gradually, to re-establish the system of multilateral trade crippled in the 1930s. One of the most useful measures here was the European Payments Union (EPU) set up with the help of a contribution of $400 million from the Americans in 1950. This allowed each country to match its debits and credits with all the others by a single payment, irrespective of the state of any bilateral payments balance, and without endangering its precious dollar holdings or earnings.

The Marshall Plan also had its limitations, however. For one thing, much of its driving force was a negative one, hostility to an outside enemy. It became part of the apparatus of the 'Cold War', the division of much of the world into two hostile camps which dominated the quarter-century after the Second World War, and contributed its share towards it. Henceforth Europe came to mean the western part of the continent and 'European' integration helped to perpetuate the gulf between East and West: it meant division as well as aggregation.

Moreover, the military and economic alliances concluded under American leadership were of the traditional type: they were temporary associations of sovereign states, reserving their own powers of ultimate decision. Thus although NATO had a nominally unified command under an American general, the French had no difficulty in withdrawing their forces and their bases from it when they so desired. There was no fundamental difference here from the system of alliances which had torn Europe apart in the past.

These developments fulfilled important functions. No doubt they helped to preserve the peace in Europe for over a quarter of a century; they conformed to the expectations above all of the Americans, but also the British and the Scandinavians; and the economic progress and full employment which took place under their shelter contributed to an easing of economic warfare between European states, to a reversion to the more relaxed economic relationships of the pre-1914 years, and consequently to encouraging once more the growth of economic interdependence. They certainly dominated the European scene in the early post-war years, but many of those who had been through the searing experience of the war and had lived in the post-war European wasteland, who had witnessed the destruction and the follies preceding it, were not satisfied to return merely to a form of business as usual. With so many of the traditional political landmarks gone after 1945, the underlying economic logic of Europe had a chance to reassert itself more powerfully. It was out of a mixture of idealistic sentiment, as well as political and economic hard-headedness and self-interest, that there emerged a new and in the long run far more significant form of economic integration, and it is this which has come increasingly to dominate the economic history of the continent of Europe in recent years.

It was in May 1950 that Robert Schuman, the French Foreign Minister, first proposed a scheme for the joint control of the French and German coal, iron and steel industries, inviting other countries to join also. The statements made by him and his associates at the time contained numerous references to ultimate political unification, and one of its objects was to make another war between Germany and France impossible, but the scheme, as proposed, was firmly anchored in concrete issues. Above all, there was the Ruhr, where Allied control had led to much friction without any clear benefits, but there was also the Saar, which had changed its political status twice between 1945 and 1949, and there was Lorraine and other coal and iron districts where repeated boundary changes had in the past led to needless waste, duplication and inefficiency. The French invitation was taken up not only by Germany, but also by Belgium, the Netherlands and Luxembourg, which had formed a customs union (Benelux) among themselves in 1948, and by Italy, which had signed a customs union treaty with France in 1949, though it had not yet been ratified. Within a year the European Coal and Steel Community (ECSC) Treaty was signed by these six countries, and in 1952 it was ratified. It came into operation in 1953.

The ECSC was an international association of a new type, and from small beginnings it quickly developed a momentum and a logic of its own. There was still a Council of Ministers to represent the six countries as independent sovereign units in negotiations, and there was a Court of Justice to adjudicate between the parties, but there was also a 'High Authority' to represent the ECSC as a whole, with its own staff developing a loyalty to the supranational authority, and with its own revenue.

Its basic aim was to create a free common market within the Six for coal, iron ore, steel and associated materials, so that production and investment could proceed in the most suitable and efficient plants anywhere within the area. Four of the six countries produced coal and all of them produced steel, but none had their coal and iron-ore deposits in the right proportions. The first step, to abolish tariffs and export subsidies, was relatively easy, and trade in the commodities covered by the treaty between the Six increased spectacularly. But it soon became clear that prices and investment decisions could still be distorted by other discrimination, as for example in rail freight rates, social-security payments or taxation practices. To resolve these in the

75 International marketing exemplified in advertisements for: the British Leyland Mini in Germany; the German Opel Rekord II in Britain; the Italian Fiat 126 in France; the French Renault 6 in Italy; the German Mercedes in France; and the Dutch DAF and the Swedish Volvo in Britain. ▶

OPEL REKORD II

"Smooth, quiet and quick." (MOTOR)

REKORD

Die Engländer haben viele Plätze, wo Tradition und ...ritt ein *date* haben. Und meist ist ein ungewöhnliches Auto dabei: ...r MINI von British Leyland.

ALORS, J'AI DESSINÈ POUR TOI LA FIAT 126.

ho trovato la nuova Renault 6, è nuovo anche lo spazio in più.

Votre première Mercedes... dès cette année...

So, if by the time you get back to the showroom you're reluctant to hand your test car back, don't be surprised.
It happens all the time.

DAF puts you automatically ahead

Even in the showroom it leaves other cars standing.

NBH 202L

MLO 7L

COULD YOU TRUST YOUR FAMILY'S SAFETY IN ANYTHING BUT A VOLVO?

A man who buys a performance car buys it for how fast it goes.
Not how fast it stops. When it comes to your family—how fast it stops really counts.
That's one of the reasons why more people are buying Volvos.
The Volvo has two independent braking systems. So, whatever the conditions,

spirit of the original agreement was not easy and the early years of the ECSC were marked by much hard bargaining. The significant fact to emerge, however, was that these difficulties did not lead to a centrifugal tendency to break up the organization, but on the contrary to a growing conviction that the alignment had to be extended from coal and steel to other commodities and to general economic and social policies. By 1955 this conclusion had become clear enough to induce Jean Monnet, architect of France's post-war economic plan and, in a major way, of the ECSC, to leave the latter in order to devote himself to its massive extension. Support for this move was by no means unanimous, but within a matter of months the foreign ministers of the Six, meeting in Messina, approved the creation of a common market in principle. The Treaty of Rome was signed in 1957, inaugurating the European Economic Community (EEC), the basis of the ultimate common market among the Six.

The nature of the drive behind this extension from free trade in a few commodities to free trade for all should be noted. There was, on the one hand, the idealism for a European future, and memory of the closely shared horrors and sufferings of war, and the decline in the belief in old-fashioned exclusive nationalism. But there was also, on the other hand, a reassertion of the logic of European industrial collaboration which had become overlaid by reasons of state from the 1870s, and there was the independent momentum of the newly established international civil service with its new loyalty, and the various economic interests and pressure groups that were learning to live with it, manipulate it and benefit from it. Conversely, it should be observed how a scheme which began as a limited customs and tariff arrangement for a handful of commodities turned, by apparently inevitable steps, into one affecting all aspects of economic and social life, to lead, ultimately, to an undermining of the traditional concept of the sovereignty of the nation-state itself.

There was little that was either spectacular or inspiring in these drives to integration, but though they were obscure and slow, they were enduring, because in the end they were based on a more realistic form of enlightened self-interest. In other words, they seemed to pay off. They were also fortunate to coincide with a wave of prosperity and expansion which could easily be attributed to the new arrangements, though any such causal connection was by no means proven or easy to quantify. In fact the economies of the Six had been growing fast and had become increasingly integrated by mutual trade well before the EEC began to operate. In any case, the tariff reductions in the early years were slow and marginal. But their increase year by year, and the expectation of a wholly free market, helped to add the momentum of integration to that of existing economic growth.

Basically the Treaty of Rome provided for complete free trade without discrimination between the six countries and for a common tariff against the rest of the world. Similarly, all restrictive quotas between them were to be abolished. This was to be achieved in a series of steps, which in fact were accelerated so that complete integration took place by 1967. The common external tariff was also harmonized by steps, settling approximately at the average level of the six constituent tariff lists, by the same date. But the intention behind the EEC was far more ambitious than these limited goals, as was made clear in Article I of the Treaty of Rome which defined its objective as

'the achievement of a harmonious development of the economy within the whole community, a continuous and balanced economic expansion, increased economic stability, a more rapid improvement in living standards, and closer relations between the member-countries.'

Almost at once capital movements were freed, and in fact some firms had anticipated the Common Market by forming associations with former competitors across the frontiers. There was also a common policy evolved on cartels and monopolies, to the effect of broadly permitting cartels but prohibiting undue control of markets by a single monopoly. An investment bank was also set up with an initial capital of $1,000 million to finance projects in underdeveloped regions, and support industries difficult to finance from one country, or of interest to several member states.

Equally, social policy had to be harmonized, to prevent any discrimination or distortion of costs which might hide behind its national differences. The freedom of migration was established in three major steps: in 1961, when the right to work in another country was granted provided no local labour was available; in 1964, when that right was made unconditional, except in special circumstances; and in 1968, when it included equal rights to social-security benefits, trade-union membership, access to public housing, vocational re-training and similar provisions.

The abolition of tedious passport formalities at the frontiers is one of the most striking consequences for the new Europe, but in fact

163

77 A cartoon ridiculing the agricultural prices policy adopted by the Common Market countries, 1973.

migration of labour among the Six turned out to be much smaller than is commonly believed, and most of it originated outside the Common Market and was therefore not affected by these changes, as is evident from the following tabulation:

Member country	Approx. annual immigration ('000) of labour in the 1960s		Total foreign labour ('000) employed 1968–70	
	From within EEC	Total	From within EEC	Total
Belgium	12	35	117	208
France	20	250	262	1,158
West Germany	150	400	477	1,839
Italy	2	4	10	33
Luxembourg	7	9	11	33
Netherlands	6	25	23	80

Apart from Luxembourg, the foreign labour even in the largest immigrant country, Germany, amounted to only 8·5 per cent of the labour force, though illegal immigrants would no doubt increase the actual figure. The main reason for these relatively low figures of labour migration is the similarity in work opportunities, in living standards, and in the rise in living standards in all the associated states (except for southern Italy), and the consequent absence of any strong incentive to move. The migrant population came mostly from the poorer countries with fewer job opportunities outside the EEC, such as Spain, Portugal, Yugoslavia and Turkey. It is a striking reminder of the fact that the new integrated Europe embraces only that part of it which makes up the old industrialized heartland. Nevertheless, despite

165

◀ 76 A selection of Europa postage stamps issued in 1973.

the relatively small-scale immigration within the EEC, the significance of its freedom should not be underrated.

Among the economic aspects of the Common Market, agriculture was probably the most difficult and controversial to co-ordinate. Before 1957, agriculturists had required subsidies in all countries, but they had been supported in different ways and to a different extent in each. Negotiations towards a common policy were both protracted and acrimonious; at one stage, in 1965–66, France in effect withdrew from EEC meetings on its account for six months, creating the most serious crisis to date among the Six. The policies finally adopted involved large levies on imports to be redistributed for the benefit of farmers, and they combined the disadvantages of high costs to consumers with the production of unwanted surpluses while still keeping farmers poorer than the rest of society. But because of a common fund, and the insistence on a common price level (which does not obtain for manufactured goods), the agricultural policies are among those which have tended most to unify the economies of the Six.

In transport, apart from the abolition of discrimination and the obvious co-ordination of time-tables, progress towards integration has been slower than might have been expected. Freight rates are still dissimilar, common legislation in such matters as long-distance road haulage is only now being debated, and the ambitious plans for important through routes, like the Brussels–Paris motorway or a system of standard-gauge canals, naturally take a long time to come to fruition. Taxation, being one of the more significant aspects of sovereignty, would be among the last measures to be co-ordinated, but a first step has been taken in the unification of turnover and purchase taxes into a single system of value-added tax, applied in a similar way in all member countries. Further progress along these lines, as also in monetary policy with an ultimate view to a common European currency is now being seriously debated and show the extent to which economic integration has already proceeded.

Less success has been achieved in the creation of a common atomic energy programme (EURATOM) agreed on at the time of the Treaty of Rome, and in common research efforts: member countries appear to prefer to devote most of their resources to their own research centres. Similarly, regional policies have not yet got off the ground, mainly because of French opposition.

While these specific aspects of Common Market policy deserve attention, however, it has become clear that what is of greater long-term importance than any particular tariff cut or any particular common fund, is the cumulative impact of their combined growth. Thus it may well be argued that what distinguishes in the most fundamental way the EEC from earlier alliances and associations (except for those which ultimately became nation states) is that a body of legislation has been built up, to which the members are bound and which they cannot any longer repeal by unilateral action as independent states. This may be only a 'functional' and therefore partial loss of sovereignty, but it is a real and potent one none the less.

Another feature which distinguishes the Rome Treaty from others in the past is its openness to new members, emphasizing that for once, it is a treaty not directed *against* any outsider. The colonies of the member states (mainly France) became 'associates' at once on free-trade terms. Greece and Turkey have also achieved associate status, and a more extensive 'association' with Mediterranean countries, mainly for freer trade, is under discussion.

Britain, among others, was invited to adhere to the Treaty of Rome in 1957, but turned down the invitation. At that time, the enormous growth potential of the continental countries compared with the British economic stagnation had not yet become clear. Nor had there been a traumatic experience in the British past to make it possible for any government to obtain popular support for a move to relinquish some political independence, and to cut the links with the Commonwealth in favour of links with other countries, two of which had been enemies in the last war. Instead, Britain proposed a free trade association. This would have led to the ending of all trading restrictions and tariffs among the members, while leaving each free to levy its own tariff rates against imports from outside, and, more importantly, it would have no implication for a continuous movement towards further integration. The Six rejected this proposal, fearing rightly that it would inhibit their own more ambitious plans, but it found favour among Sweden, Switzerland and Austria, each unwilling to risk its neutral status by joining a potential alliance, as well as Denmark, Norway and Portugal, and in 1959 the Seven formed the European Free Trade Association (EFTA). Finland joined in 1961.

While EFTA made less sense than EEC, from the point of view of both geographical and economic complementarity, its internal tariff reductions proceeded at the same pace as those of the EEC and some trade was generated or diverted as a result and a larger market created. Nevertheless, the fast-expanding Common Market proved an

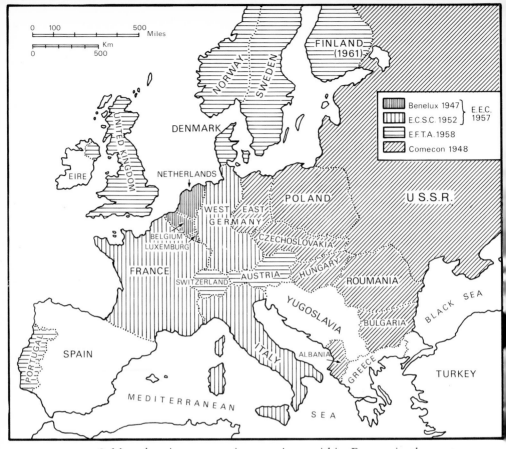

78 Map showing economic groupings within Europe in the post-war period; Britain, Denmark and Eire entered the Common Market on 1 January 1973.

irresistible magnet, and Britain applied for membership in 1961–63 and again in 1966–67. On both occasions her entry was prevented by the French veto, but she was successful in 1972. With her, Denmark and the Republic of Ireland entered, Norway having decided by a last-minute plebiscite to stay out, so that the Common Market became one of nine countries from 1 January 1973, with a growing number of associated areas.

Whatever the future of the enlarged economic community, it cannot be denied that it marked a new phase in the history of European economic integration, representing a much greater step towards a single economy, and a much higher level of industrial potential of the areas concerned than ever before. At the same time, even with Britain and the other two new members, the Europe included in it is a very limited Europe indeed.

In one respect the political map of Europe after 1945 has been less favourable to a common European development than that of the inter-war years: the Soviet Union, continuing to pursue her own form of industrialization largely in isolation from the West, has pushed her frontiers forward, approximately to those of the former Tsarist Empire, while several more countries have joined her in preferring the Soviet-type planned and directed economy to the western model. They have formed their own regional economic association (COMECON) to institutionalize their natural preference to trade with each other and co-ordinate their development. At present it is not yet clear whether that economic development will take a shape very similar to that of the West, despite the fundamental political and social differences, whether it will take an entirely different shape, or whether the East will be left behind in economic stagnation. Most indications point to the first of those possibilities.

It should be stressed that, with some significant exceptions, the regions covered by COMECON belong to the very late indus-trializers in Europe and not to its industrial heartland whose outlines have not changed much in the past 100–150 years. They are therefore not very different from the other peripheral areas of 1860, most of which are also still peripheral, showing rising incomes and some mechanization, but still unable to bridge the gap that separates them from the industrialized countries. They include Greece, Turkey, southern Italy, Spain, Portugal and Ireland. The contrast between much the same economically advanced and retarded regions in the twentieth century as in the eighteenth, surviving two centuries of industrialization, points to something enduring in the structure of Europe. It may well be that the economic logic which demands the integration of at least the advanced areas will prove equally durable and powerful. At the same time, it also poses the question as to the future relationship with the less favoured continents, at a time when 15 per cent of the world's population, many of them in Europe, enjoy 70–80 per cent of the world's wealth and income.

Will the European economic miracle continue? We cannot foretell the future. We cannot guarantee prosperity or full employment, nor the maintenance of social peace under a benign phase of capitalism. Many human needs are not being met today, even in the most advanced countries, while the less fortunate nations, still caught in a trap of poverty and slow growth, cry out for justice. Nor have we properly tested the efficiency with which western society can eliminate the ill-effects of the pollution and ecological unbalance it is creating.

In 1907 a German economist, Sartorius von Waltershausen, published a perceptive study of foreign investment, in which he posed, in a different form, some of the same questions:

'Truly, Europe poses the greatest enigma as to her political and economic future. Do not we see how the members of the various nations come together ever more frequently and in growing numbers, in journeys and meetings, for purposes of business and culture, how they try to understand each other, try to learn from each other, that the races of neighbouring countries are becoming more and more mixed by migration and marriage, that no great work of science, technology or art is born which does not rapidly become the common property of Europe, that the deep need for a new content of life, for new ethical and religious aims occupies the thinkers of all countries in similar fashion, while everywhere the old belief of the medieval past is being dissolved by contemporary knowledge . . .? [Yet] who can shut himself off from the events of the present: Norway has separated from Sweden because of a deep divergence, Hungary wants to tear herself away from Austria as far as her commercial policies are concerned, the Polish question has become a new threat to Germany, in Russia the age-old hostilities of race and nation have emerged again during the Revolution [of 1905]. And then the armaments on land and at sea, the commercial envy by England of the industrial rise of Germany, the struggle for the domination of Africa, the endless troubles in the Balkan peninsula!

Is not the life of Europe today the cry of a terrible contradiction, the great mystery of a harmonious yet at the same time divisive process of evolution?'

Seven years after this was written, the First World War broke out – to confirm the author's worst fears and to belie his hopes. We cannot, perhaps, be any more optimistic today and we may be equally puzzled. All we can say, with some measure of confidence, is that of the two choices, the path of collaboration and integration fits more happily and more easily into the process of industrialization which began in Europe two centuries ago and of which there is no end in sight.

SELECT BIBLIOGRAPHY

GENERAL WORKS ON INDUSTRIALIZATION AND
INTEGRATION
Ashworth, William *A Short History of the
International Economy, 1850–1950* (London,
1952)
Bairoch, Paul *Révolution industrielle et sous-
développement* (Paris, 1964)
Heaton, Herbert *Economic History of Europe*
(New York, 1964)
Henderson, W.O. *Genesis of the Common
Market* (London, 1962)
Hoffman, W.G. *The Growth of Industrial
Economies* (Manchester, 1958)
Hughes, J.R.T. *Industrialization and Economic
History* (New York, 1970)
Kemp, Tom *Industrialization in Nineteenth
Century Europe* (London, 1969)
Kenwood, A.G. and Lougheed, A.L. *The
Growth of the International Economy, 1820–
1960* (London, 1971)
Landes, David S. *The Unbound Prometheus*
(Cambridge, 1969)
Pollard, S. and Holmes, C. *Documents of
European Economic History* (3 vols, London,
1968–73)
Woodruff, William *The Emergence of an
International Economy, 1700–1914*, Fontana
Economic History of Europe, IV, section 11
(London, 1971)

TRADE AND INDUSTRIALIZATION
Berrill, Kenneth 'International Trade and the
Rate of Economic Growth', *Economic History
Review*, 2nd series, XII/3 (1960)
Clark, Colin *The Conditions of Economic Pro-
gress* (London, 1957)
Condliffe, J.B. *The Commerce of Nations* (Lon-
don, 1951)
Deutsch, Karl and Eckstein, Alexander
'National Industrialization and the Declining
Share of the International Economic Sector',
World Politics, XIII/2 (1961)
Hughes, J.R.T. 'Foreign Trade and Balanced
Growth: The Historical Framework', *Ameri-
can Economic Review*, Suppl. (1959)

Kindleberger, C.P. 'Foreign Trade and Eco-
nomic Growth: Lessons from Britain and
France, 1850–1913', *Economic History Review*,
2nd series, XIV/2 (1961)
—— *Foreign Trade and the National Economy*
(New Haven, Conn., 1962)
Kuznets, Simon 'Quantitative Aspects of the
Economic Growth of Nations. X, Level and
Structure of Foreign Trade: Long-Term
Trends', *Economic Development and Cultural
Change*, XV/2, part II (1967)
Maizels, Alfred *Industrial Growth and World
Trade* (Cambridge, 1963)
Nurkse, Ragnar *Patterns of Trade and Develop-
ment* (Stockholm, 1959)
Ohlin, Bertil *Interregional and International
Trade* (Cambridge, Mass., 1933)
Thorp, Willard Long *Business Annals* (New
York, 1926)
Tyszynski, H. 'World Trade in Manufactured
Commodities, 1899–1950', *Manchester School*,
XIX/3 (1951)
Weckstein, Richard S. (ed.) *Expansion of World
Trade and the Growth of National Economies*
(New York, 1968)
Wilson, C.H. 'The Growth of Overseas Com-
merce and European Manufacture', *New
Cambridge Modern History*, VII (Cambridge,
1957)

TRANSPORT AND COMMUNICATIONS
Fayle, C. Ernest *A Short History of the World's
Shipping Industry* (London, 1933)
Hennig, Richard *Die Hauptwege des Weltverkehrs*
(Jena, 1913)
Jagtiani, H.M. *The Role of the State in the Pro-
vision of Railways* (London, 1924)
Middleton, P.H. *Railways of Thirty Nations*
(New York, 1937)
North, Douglass 'Ocean Freight Rates and
Economic Development, 1750–1913', *Journal
of Economic History*, XVIII (1958)
Weithase, Hugo *Geschichte des Weltpostvereins*
(Strasbourg, 1895)

MIGRATION OF LABOUR

Berthoff, R.T. *British Immigrants in Industrial America, 1790–1950* (Cambridge, Mass., 1953)

Ferenczi, Imre and Willcox, Walter F. *International Migrations* (New York, vol. 1, 1929, vol. 2, 1931)

Henderson, W.O. *Britain and Industrial Europe, 1750–1870* (Liverpool, 1954)

Ladame, Paul Alexis *Le rôle des migrations dans le monde libre* (Paris, 1958)

Moller, Herbert (ed.) *Population Movements in Modern European History* (New York and London, 1964)

Scott, F.D. (ed.) *World Migration in Modern Times* (Englewood Cliffs, N.J., 1968)

Walker, Mack *Germany and the Emigration, 1816–1885* (Cambridge, Mass., 1964)

MIGRATION OF CAPITAL

Cameron, Rondo E. *France and the Economic Development of Europe, 1800–1914* (Princeton, N.J., 1961)

——'L'exportation des capitaux français, 1850–1880', *Revue d'Histoire Economique et Sociale*, 33 (1955)

—— 'Some French Contributions to the Industrial Development of Germany, 1840–1870', *Journal of Economic History*, XVI/3 (1956)

Crisp, Olga 'French Investments in Russian Joint-Stock Companies, 1894–1914', *Business History*, II (1960)

Feis, Herbert *Europe, The World's Banker, 1870–1914* (New Haven, Conn., 1930)

Gille, Bertrand *Banking and Industrialization in Europe, 1730–1914*, Fontana Economic History of Europe, III, section 4 (London, 1970)

——*La Banque et le crédit en France de 1815 à 1848* (Paris, 1959)

Hall, A.R. (ed.) *The Export of Capital from Britain, 1870–1914* (London, 1968)

Hobson, C.K. *The Export of Capital* (London, 1914)

Jenks, Leland H. *The Migration of British Capital to 1875* (New York, 1963)

Landes, David S. 'The Old Bank and the New: The Financial Revolution of the Nineteenth Century', in F. Crouzet, W.H. Chaloner and W.M. Stern (ed.) *Essays in European Economic History, 1789–1914* (London, 1969)

Lévy-Leboyer, Maurice *Les banques européennes et l'industrialisation internationale dans la première moitié du XIXe siècle* (Paris, 1964)

Segal, Harvey H. and Simon, Matthew 'British

Foreign Capital Issues, 1865–1894', *Journal of Economic History*, XXI (1961)

Waltershausen, Sartorius von *Das volkswirtschaftliche System der Kapitalanlage im Auslande* (Berlin, 1907)

White, Harry D. *The French International Accounts, 1880–1913* (Cambridge, Mass., 1933)

EUROPE AND OVERSEAS DEVELOPMENT

Clark, G. *The Balance Sheets of Imperialism* (New York, 1967)

Gollwitzer, Heinz *Europe in the Age of Imperialism, 1880–1918* (London and New York, 1969)

Hobson, J.A. *Imperialism, a Study* (London, 1902)

Koebner, R. and Schmidt, H.D. *Imperialism, the Story and Significance of a Political Word, 1840–1960* (Cambridge, 1964)

New Cambridge Modern History Vol. XII: *The Era of Violence* (Cambridge, 1960)

Semmel, Bernard *The Rise of Free Trade Imperialism* (Cambridge, 1970)

Snyder, L.L. (ed.) *The Imperialism Reader* (Princeton, N.J., 1962)

Taylor, A.J.P. *The Struggle for Mastery in Europe, 1848–1918* (Oxford, 1954)

Viallate, Achille *Economic Imperialism and International Relations during the Last Fifty Years* (New York, 1923)

Woodruff, William *Impact of Western Man* (London, 1966)

TREATIES, TARIFFS AND CUSTOMS UNIONS

Ashley, Percy *Modern Tariff History* (London, 1910)

Dunham, Arthur Louis *The Anglo-French Treaty of Commerce of 1860 and the Progress of the Industrial Revolution in France* (Ann Arbor, Mich., 1930)

Gerschenkron, Alexander *Bread and Democracy in Germany* (New York, 1966)

Henderson, W.O. *The Zollverein* (London, 1959)

Luzzatto, Gino 'The Italian Economy in the First Decade after Unification', in F. Crouzet, W.H. Chaloner and W.M. Stern (ed.) *Essays in European Economic History, 1789–1914* (London, 1969)

Price, Arnold H. *The Evolution of the Zollverein* (Ann Arbor, Mich., 1949)

Weber, W. *Der deutsche Zollverein* (Leipzig, 1871)

Willis, Henry Parker *A History of the Latin Monetary Union* (Chicago, Ill., 1903)

ECONOMIC DISINTEGRATION, 1914–1945

Ellsworth, P. T. *The International Economy, its Structure and Operation* (New York, 1950)

Gordon, Margaret S. *Barriers to World Trade. A Study of Recent Commercial Policy* (New York, 1941)

League of Nations *Commercial Policy in the Inter-War Period* (Geneva, 1942)

League of Nations *International Currency Experience: Lessons of the Inter-War Period* (Geneva, 1944)

Plummer, Alfred *International Combines in Modern Industry* (London, 1934)

Roepke, Wilhelm *International Economic Disintegration* (London, 1942)

Rowe, J. W. F. *Markets and Men. A Study of Artificial Control Schemes in Some Primary Industries* (Cambridge, 1936)

Royal Institute of International Affairs *World Agriculture, an International Survey* (London, 1932)

Svennilson, Ingvar *Growth and Stagnation in the European Economy* (Geneva, 1954)

EUROPE, POST-1945

Barraclough, Geoffrey *European Unity in Thought and Action* (Oxford, 1963)

Camps, Miriam *European Unification in the Sixties* (New York, 1966, and London, 1967)

Dell, Sydney *Trade Blocs and Common Markets* (London, 1963)

Patterson, G. *Discrimination in International Trade, the Policy Issues, 1945–1965* (Princeton, N.J., 1966)

Postan, M. M. *An Economic History of Western Europe, 1945–1964* (London, 1967)

Robson, Peter (ed.) *International Economic Integration* (Harmondsworth, 1972)

Roepke, Wilhelm *International Order and Economic Integration* (Dordrecht, 1959)

Tew, Brian *International Monetary Co-operation* (London, 1960)

Walsh, A. E. and Paxton, John *The Structure and Development of the Common Market* (London, 1968)

Yeager, L. B. *International Monetary Relations* (New York, 1966)

LIST OF ILLUSTRATIONS

19 Advertisement by a Leipzig importer for American tinned goods, in *Kladderadatsch*, Berlin, 1870; British Museum, London.

20 Cartoon on German agricultural tariffs, in *Kladderadatsch*, Berlin, 1879; British Museum, London.

21 Railway station at Rendsburg, Prussia; painting by Carl Ross, 1846; Railway Museum, Copenhagen.

22 Handkerchief with printed design commemorating the first appearance of steamboats on the Rhine in 1832; Musée de l'Impression sur Etoffe, Mulhouse.

23 The Rhône–Danube canal and the railway at Erlangen, engraving, 1845; Deutsches Museum, Munich.

24 Heading of the first number of *Le Chemin de Fer*, Brussels, 1841; British Museum, London.

25 Goods and cattle trains on the Liverpool and Manchester Railway, 1831; detail of aquatint by S. Hughes after a drawing by J. Shaw, from a series 'Travelling on the Liverpool and Manchester Railway', published by Ackermann & Co., London, 1831; British Museum, London.

26 A Paris–Nancy goods train, and passengers at a station, *c.* 1850, print published by Pinot, Epinal; photo Giraudon.

27 Map of railway systems to 1877; drawing by S. Schotten.

28 The opening of a railway line in Russia, print published in Moscow, 1857; British Museum, London.

29 Building the Trans-Siberian Railway; after a painting in the Historical Museum, Moscow.

30 Advertisement by Burgeff & Co., liqueur manufacturers, Hochheim-on-Main, in *Jugend*, Munich, 1905.

31 Lithograph by Honoré Daumier, in *La Caricature*, No. 20, 1831; British Museum, London.

32 'The Paris Bourse', cartoon by Gustave Doré, in *Le Journal pour Rire*, Paris, 1851.

33 ' "If this God did not exist he would have to be invented" – Voltaire, ex-capitalist', cartoon by Bertall, Paris, 1847; British Museum, London.

34 'Money is the bridge between nations', cartoon by Bertall, Paris, 1847; British Museum, London.

35 Title-page of *Das Haus Rothschild* by I.L. Kober, Prague and Leipzig, 1858; British Museum, London.

36 'The Redeemer from the east', cartoon in *Deutsche Brusseler Zeitung*, Frankfurt-on-Main, 1848; Staatsbibliothek, Berlin.

37 'Moritz von Bethmann and Anselm Meyer Rothschild as the coachmen of Europe', cartoon by A.E. Schalk, in *Bilder aus Frankfurt*, No. 1, 1850; Stadt und Universitätsbibliothek, Frankfurt-on-Main.

38 'The Bubble burst', drawing by George Cruikshank, 1825; British Museum, London.

39 Railway promoters submitting bills for parliamentary discussion, cartoon in *Illustrated London News*, November, 1845.

40 'Lord Brougham's railway nightmare', cartoon in *Punch*, 1845; British Museum, London.

41 Factory of the Société Anonyme des Mines et Fonderies de la Vieille Montagne, Oberhausen, lithograph by Canelle, Brussels, 1852; British Museum, London.

42 'Monsieur Mercure, associate of a powerful bank', cartoon by Bertall, Paris, 1847; British Museum, London.

43 'Panic at the Paris Bourse', lithograph by Honoré Daumier, 1844; British Museum, London.

44 France paying her indemnity to Germany, cartoon in *Kladderadatsch*, Berlin, 1871; British Museum, London.

45 'The Fight for the Foot-plate', cartoon in *Punch*, 1899; British Museum, London.

46 'The New Loan', cartoon in *Borsszem Jankó*, Pest, 1873; British Museum, London.

47 Advertisement by the Russian-American India Rubber Co., in a banking and trade calendar, St Petersburg, 1912; British Museum, London.

48 The Cockerill works at Seraing, Belgium, lithograph by E. Toovey, Brussels, 1852; British Museum, London.

49 Steelworks at Lendersdorf, painting by C. Schütz, 1838; Leopold Hoesch Museum, Düren.

50 Drawings of the Bell Rock Lighthouse, by Charles Dupin, in *Voyage dans la Grande Bretagne*, Paris, 1824; British Museum, London.

51 Manchester cotton mills, 1826, drawing from the diary of C. F. Schinkel, published in his *Reisetagebücher*, 1863–64; British Museum, London.

52 'Italian industry has opened yet another door for itself', cartoon in *Jugend*, Munich, 1906; British Museum, London.

53 Title-page of *Der Welthandel*, Stuttgart, 1869; British Museum, London.

54 'Levelling and making out the line', illustration from *Account of the Electric Telegraph and Railway for Chitchen and Gramup People in Punjabi*, Amritsar, 1865; India Office Library, London.

55 *Gold digging at Ararat*, painting by J. Roper, 1854; Dixson Galleries, Sydney.

56 Packing tea for export in India, engraving from E. Ukhtomsky, *Travels in the East of Nicholas II*, 1895–96; British Museum, London.

57 Advertisement by the Compañia Colonial, Madrid, 1868; British Museum, London.

58 Advertisement for tea and rum, in *Borsszem Jankó*, Pest, 1868; British Museum, London.

59 'How Lord Roberts wrote Bovril', advertisement, 1900; British Museum, London.

60 'Hold on John', cartoon in *Punch*, 1898; British Museum, London.

61 'Wooing the African Venus', cartoon in *Punch*, 1888; British Museum, London.

62 General view of the Paris Universal Exhibition, 1867, lithograph by Deroy; photo Roger-Viollet.

63 The Nuremberg–Fürth railway, 1835, watercolour by an unknown artist; Georg Schäfer Collection, Schweinfurt.

64 Map of Europe in 1914, published in Dresden; Imperial War Museum, London.

65 Cartoon on the effect of the Tariff Act of 1879, in *Kladderadatsch*, Berlin, 1879; British Museum, London.

66 Laying cables at Cologne for the underground telegraph system, painting by Christian Sell, 1880; courtesy, Cologne Chamber of Commerce.

67 *Speculators*, drawing by Otto Dix, 1923; Private Collection.

68 Map of Europe in 1919; drawing by Gillian D. March.

69 *The Match-seller*, painting by Otto Dix, 1921; Staatsgalerie, Stuttgart.

70 Cartoon on the economic crisis, in *Simplizissimus*, Munich, 1931; British Museum, London.

71 *In front of the Labour Exchange*, painting by Grete Jürgens, 1929; Niedersächsische Landesgalerie, Hanover.

72 Nazi election poster, 1930; Victoria and Albert Museum, London.

73 Cartoon on protectionist tariffs by J. Braakensiek, in *Groene Amsterdamer*, Amsterdam, 1931.

74 Marshall Plan poster, 1950, designed by Gaston van den Eynde; Victoria and Albert Museum, London.

75 Collage of advertisements for motor cars manufactured by British Leyland; DAF (Netherlands); Fiat (Italy); Opel and Mercedes (Germany); Renault (France); and Volvo (Sweden).

76 Selection of postage stamps issued in 1973; courtesy, Stanley Gibbons Ltd; photo R. B. Fleming.

77 Cartoon on Common Market agricultural prices policy, in *European Community*, Brussels, 1973.

78 Map showing post-war economic groupings in Europe; drawing by Gillian D. March.

All illustrations from publications in the British Museum and the Victoria and Albert Museum were photographed by J. R. Freeman & Co.

INDEX